SCALED
AGILE
IMPLEMENTATIONS

D1564137

SCALED AGILE IMPLEMENTATIONS

Agile Applications Beyond IT

by

ANUSHA HEWAGE

To My Mother

ABOUT THE AUTHOR

Anusha is the founder of AgiltyDNA, which provides advocacy to enterprises and leaders who are keen to implement Agile at enterprise levels.

She has previously worked in many multinational companies, including Emirates Airlines, 3M, Accenture, IBM, and General Electric. She has provided leadership to some of the biggest Agile and business transformation initiatives for customers in banking, insurance, aviation, oil & gas, not-for profit, media & entertainment, and more than 15 startups in different countries.

She is specialized in various Agile frameworks like the Scaled Agile framework, Large scale scrum, Nexus, Kanban, Disciplined Agile, Scrum and experiments and does research in the Agile way of working in non-IT settings. Her research and empirical studies have led her to write a few other books in Agile, including 'Becoming a Great Scrum Master', 'Becoming an Awesome Product Owner' and 'Anti-Agile Patterns'.

She engages with the readers of her books and continues to support them in the Agile transformation journey. Readers can contact her through www.AgilityDNA.com or through the email address AgilityDNA@gmail.com.

TABLE OF CONTENTS

INTRODUCTION

Twenty-one years have passed since the Agile Manifesto was written in 2001. It proposed changes on how software is built. Since then, the Agile way of working has been used in the IT industry and has made incremental but steady progress.

The Agile way of working is an integral part of the software building process. It would be fair to say that Agile has made IT an extremely successful industry. The proof of this success is that three companies out of ten in the Fortune 100 company list in 2021 are tech companies (Apple, Amazon, Alphabet). Surprisingly, none of these companies existed 30 years ago. The other interesting fact is that immediately after the COVID-19 outbreak in 2019, the IT industry was one of the few industries that started booming and was least impacted by the global paralysis.

While the Agile way of working is not the only factor contributing to this success, it has enabled the IT industry to develop a mindset that can easily adapt, shifting focus to respond to changes quickly. As a result, IT companies or IT departments are progressing at a steady pace. However, IT departments are sometimes hindered by other business units still working in traditional ways. Such business units are slow and reluctant to change.

The 15th annual State of Agile report compiled by digital. ai (after researching more than 1,000 companies) is evidence of this.

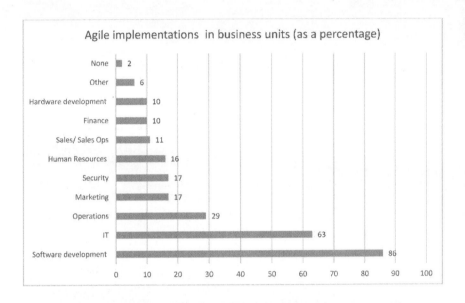

Figure 1: Agile implementations across various business units
(extract from 15th annual State of Agile Report, digital.ai)

Some business units take progressive approaches adopting Agile ways of working; however, many are not keen or reluctant to make the move. The empirical research shows that there is a correlation between the operational performance of the enterprises and Agile practices. Some of this empirical research was in unconventional areas like supply chain, marketing, or manufacturing.

As Agile practitioners who have seen how the Agile concepts and practices can help wherever they are applied, we recommend leaders adopt them in other business units and at the enterprise level. Agile application beyond team and IT division level gives unique advantages. Those who have managed to gain a firm grip on the adoption of this new way of working at business unit and enterprise levels have demonstrated competitive advantages and are market leaders in terms of financial performance. Industrial research done by McKinsey, Gartner, Forbes, etc., has identified enterprise/business Agile capabilities as deal breakers and essential capabilities companies should invest in for the future. Adoption of these practices by other business units and ultimately at the enterprise level is becoming mandatory.

However, there is a difference between 'doing' Agile and 'being' Agile. In doing Agile, Agile is just another process and another method the organization and teams adopt when required. But being Agile is a culture. It is fundamentally a way everyone in the organization thinks and acts. It applies to everyone from C-level to the lowest level of the organization.

The leaders who try to 'be Agile' change their operating behaviors and leadership styles. As an example, a COO of a bank that started using Agile at leadership level began by giving away his corner office and hot-desking like other employees. That simple behavioral change allowed the other employees access to him at any time and broke down the barriers between other employees and his executive office. That was a true transformation to servant leadership. The same leader started attending the program showcases and discarding monthly steering committee reviews, hence removing the unproductive steering committee preparation times for other teams and other executive leaders.

Although the Agile concept, philosophy, principles, and practices can be adopted by any level/unit of an enterprise, the wider perception about Agile is that it is only applicable to IT and only at team levels. Research suggests that leaders are skeptical about making the bold move of adopting Agile at the enterprise level and in non-IT business units. However, a few trailblazers have broken this stereotype and gained significant advantages, proving that Agile is applicable at every level and unit.

The objective of this book is to provide insights and information, along with some reassuring evidence, to help business leaders planning to adopt Agile in non-IT business areas across the enterprise. Hence this book is for business leaders or new Agile practitioners who want to find out what Agile is and to which business areas it can be applied, including non-IT areas. It provides case studies and real-world business Agile applications, along with steps to start Agile across other business units beyond IT. While some of the examples are publicly available case studies from literature, most are from organizations or customers where the author was personally involved in the transformation process.

While Agile implementation and injecting this way of working into business units across enterprises will be a continuous journey, organizations can gain mastery of the process by creating their own frameworks and sometimes changing the organizational structures to truly embrace the

Agility culture. One method doesn't work for everyone, so enterprises need to invest early enough to find the best working Agile methodologies, practices, and cultural changes to prepare them for the uncertain future.

~ SECTION 1 ~

THE RATIONALE

1
WHY AGILE?

When the novel Coronavirus (COVID-19) pandemic hit the world in February 2020, it devastated the national economy of many countries. Successful companies were crippled, and governments around the world could not conduct their day-to-day business as usual. Everyone was confined to their homes instead of commuting to their offices.

COVID-19 changed many things. Ships built to sail were abandoned in harbors, and airplanes remained grounded at airports. Companies established to grow businesses and provide jobs for millions of people were forced to shut down. No person alive today has seen something of this nature.

As the pandemic bit harder, almost all industries suffered as they struggled to figure out how to maintain their cash flow. Bills piled up, and incoming cash flows dried up without an alternative source of income. Ultimately, company leaders had to make the tough decision to relieve their staff of their duties. In the aftermath of this, most companies shut down temporarily to wait for the pandemic situation to subside, but others did so permanently, filing for bankruptcy.

Despite these harsh realities, a few industries thrived during this depressing period, for example, those in the life sciences sector. The reason for this is obvious: a virus is responsible for the pandemic. Healthcare professionals were at the center of various measures taken to manage the outbreak. The marathon to find a vaccine gave an extra boost to companies involved in pioneering medical research as their share prices skyrocketed.

However, there were sweeping changes not only in the health and life sciences sectors. The information technology (IT) industry also emerged as a focal point despite appearing to have no direct correlation with COVID-19 management.

On the surface, IT is not related to healthcare or life sciences, but software engineers, data scientists, IT analysts, database architects, and security specialists — in fact, almost all IT professionals — became very in demand. During this period, some IT companies reported exponential growth within a month or two of the outbreaks. An example is the video conferencing company, Zoom, which recorded 355% revenue growth in the second quarter of 2020 (Jeremy C. Owens, Marketwatch.com, Sept 1, 2020). Other companies that experienced this unexpected growth trajectory include Amazon, Microsoft, Apple and almost all other IT-based companies. The formula was simple: As people were restricted to their homes as part of preventive measures to stop the spread of the virus, IT became the key to connection.

Many companies across the world signed up for Zoom, Microsoft Teams, Cisco Webex, and WhatsApp. Consequently, these IT companies and others recorded unexpected exponential growth rates that followed the high spike in demand. One significant factor common to these companies was their preparedness for the change. No company shut down because of their lack of capacity to accommodate the daily surge in demand from IT product users; instead, their systems were ready for the changes that were announced. For those that could not immediately accommodate the changes, reinforcements were ready within days. These categories of companies hired additional staff members. Amazon reported hiring more than 70,000 people during this period (including casual staff). Overall, these IT firms responded to the changes proactively with an astonishing speed.

We should give credit to the IT industry for being so swift and nimble. They reacted to the situation very quickly regardless of where the demand arose. In fact, the heightened demand flow during this period was multidirectional; from government authorities urgently seeking to develop contact tracing systems, from people stuck at home requiring food or medicine deliveries, and from schools and universities attempting to conduct lessons online to deliver education to children and students stuck at home.

There was also demand from everyday people tired of their mobility constraints and desperate to connect with friends and family located near and far. This was in addition to demand from research laboratories that conducted massive data-driven vaccine trials. Simply put, demand was massive, but the IT industry took up the gauntlet. Who knows what the world would have looked like during the pandemic if there were no IT experts.

But how did the IT industry do this? The answer is not that simple. Information technology is extremely complex. Let's take WhatsApp as an example. The WhatsApp mobile app that you probably use every day is the product of a series of complicated developmental processes. The app uses close coordination between many resources such as hardware, software, etc. To streamline, let's take a look at the software side of IT.

The entire logic of how software runs is highly intricate. Software is the main engine room of any technology and is normally measured through lines of code. As an example, below is a simple line of code written in a programming language called C++ (pronounced as 'C Plus Plus').

```
Float fahr;

printf("Enter Fahrenheit: ");

scanf("%f", &fahr);

printf("Celsius is %f\n", (fahr-32)*5/9);
```

This line of code (or computer instructions) will display a message on the computer screen 'Enter Fahrenheit' and wait for the user to enter a number. When the user enters a number, it converts that number to its equivalent in Celsius and displays it on the screen as well. Depending on the programming language, the number of lines required to perform the same task might vary. It could be shorter or lengthier. But think of it this way: If four lines of code are required to convert Fahrenheit to Celsius, how many lines of code would be needed to display a search result in Google?

Well, by 2015, the Google search engine had two billion lines of code. If you were to print the Google search engine code on A4 paper, it would amount to 32 million A4 sheets! Plus, this number is continually increasing as more and more functions are added to the software. So, if Google uses millions of lines of code, what about the entire Facebook application? Or Instagram? Or the mobile banking app that you use on your phone? What about the IT systems which operate at London Heathrow Terminal 5? It includes millions and billions line of coding.

The code is not the only thing IT solutions need to tackle. IT solutions also involve laptops, desktops, phones or wearables, communication devices like modems or routers, and many other infrastructure services and devices, which make IT-based solutions extremely complicated to implement.

Cost of Change and Redoing Work

Considering the number of lines of code and other infrastructural services and devices involved, changes to IT systems or solutions using them can be highly challenging. For example, adding new or deleting existing functionality is extremely complicated as such changes may trigger other subsequent changes or require the code to be rewritten yet again. Imagine an apartment complex of 40 floors, and on the 13th floor, the owner of the apartment wants to add another bedroom that extends beyond the balcony. This may sound simple, but it is not. Because the extension may change the approved building architecture, the building may require new architecture, which could mean redesigning the entire building structure. Similarly, programmers need to identify what code base should be changed and make those changes as appropriate. Then, once the updates are completed, they need to retest the entire code base and then release it to the customers so they can utilize the new features.

However, during this entire redesigning process, existing programs need to run and cannot be stopped. To give you a precise idea of how this works, you might be currently reading this book on a Kindle eBook reader. Meanwhile, at Amazon, developers may be adding or deleting new lines of code to the Kindle eBook reader. Once this is done, they will release the update to your Kindle device — sometimes you won't even notice the change has happened! Making changes to IT systems is a complex process that is both a science and an art.

Of course, such changes did not occur so efficiently until a few years ago. Previously, if new functionality was required — let's say you were a customer and you wanted Instagram in pink — then the IT guys would need a year's advance notice to make that happen. Of course, if during the waiting period you said, "Oh, I've changed my mind, I now need that to be in jet black," this would make the IT experts go berserk because they would have to rewrite the entire code again. Everything they had done till then was an utter waste of time.

In this case, the IT personnel might react in several ways. They could completely ignore your request and still give you the pink version. (Take it or leave it: you paid for it). Or they might try to convince you how nice the pink is. The third approach is that they could ask you to pay a crazy amount to implement the changes because they needed to rewrite the whole code. From their side, it was not simple, hence the huge effort estimation. If you agreed to pay the huge amount they asked for, then they would finally have to go back to their computers, rewrite the codes, and produce the jet-black version of Instagram you wanted — this might take a lot more time, which you wouldn't be happy about.

This delay and how the IT professionals behaved when asked to change direction was because of the way software was developed historically, through a method called 'Waterfall'.

The Waterfall Way of Developing Software

A few decades ago, IT used to develop products, solutions, or software in the following manner:

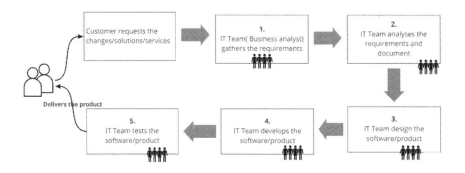

Figure 2 : Traditional software development process

This process is termed 'Waterfall' because the steps required to develop a product or solution happen one after the other.

Throughout the process, a lot of documents are created to make sure no requests or requirements from the customer are overlooked. Since the customer is not a part of the development team, the development team always ensure they understand the requirements properly in case there is a need to document or verify these requirements before the development begins. Then, along the development chain process, different engineers perform different tasks according to their area of specialization. This, therefore, means that the project is passed down from one person to another or from one function to another. Below is an example of the tasks involved in each phase and the people involved:

1. Requirement gathering	IT business analyst
2. Requirement analysis	Systems analysts
3. System design	Architects and designers
4. Development	Software engineers
5. Testing	Quality assurance engineers or testers
6. Smooth transition between each phase	The project manager or solutions manager

Table 1 : Task segregation in traditional
software development process

This linear approach has led to many surprising outcomes explained brilliantly in the illustration below (source : the project cartoon):

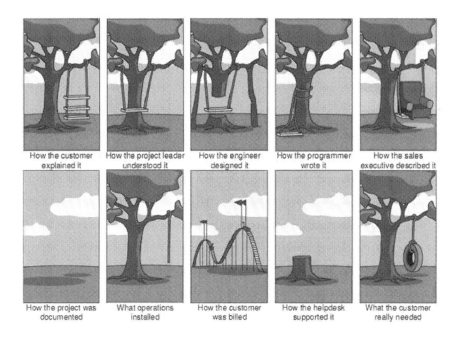

Figure 3: The misinterpretations

It is a very apt representation of what occurs with such processes. It is a nightmare when you realize there are gaps in the solution you have built. Customers may not get what they want, and development teams may spend month after month getting it right. The rejection of a finished product by the customer can be very painful for the developers and costly for the customer and investors.

The following is an exhaustive list of reasons to explain why this process is not ideal and wasteful:

- The customer who ultimately uses the product is not engaged in the process of building it and as a result their needs are not understood properly.

- The product is built upon assumptions which might prove wrong once the customer starts using it.
- Customers cannot explain the requirements in the detail that the developers need until they can start using the system.
- The IT team who develops the software is not close enough to the customer's business domain or business function to understand the customer's needs and any potential future needs.
- The intermediaries between the customer and developers translate customer requirements which might lead to miscommunications and misunderstandings.
- The software development team works in isolation, which requires a lot of handholding at each level:
  o Business analysts explain the requirements to the solution architect. The solution architect explains the planned solution to the front-end designer and software engineer. The software engineer explains how the system works to testers, and then testers explain how it is tested back to business analysts and so on. Each of them works in isolation with very little interaction, and most operate with their own SLAs.
- The software development team works on multiple projects at a time resulting in waste due to context switching.
- The software development team does not have the ownership of the process. As a consequence, the team is only passively engaged and less motivated.

- The software development team's full potential, including their leadership skills and ideas, are not fully utilized and respected. Instead, they are told what to do and how to do the work by those who do not understand the ground-level details.
- The software development team has unsustainable work processes. They are often pushed to work long hours due to changes and demanding managers who want to get the work done at cheaper costs. As a result, their personal and family lives are often compromised.

These practices lead to an unsatisfactory and demotivated working culture, which ultimately results in poor software products and dissatisfied customers. This is the reason the IT sector has experimented with new ways of working that embrace changes, as change is the only thing that is constant in software development.

Agility in IT

The Cambridge dictionary defines 'agility' as 'ways of planning and doing work in which it is understood that making changes as they are needed is an important part of the job'. In 1982, Brown and Agnew (p.29) described 'agility' in the business context as the 'capacity to react quickly to rapidly changing circumstances'. In the context of this book, 'agility' is defined as 'the ability to connect with the external and internal forces where the consumption of services exists and respond to needs and requests proactively and reactively to a satisfactory level for the benefit of everyone involved in the end-to-end process'. It can be applied to IT, any other business unit, or the entire organization. However, in the context of IT, IT agility is the ability to respond proactively and reactively to consumers' needs to their satisfaction. Consumers are other organizations, departments, or the general public, like you and me.

In the past, IT struggled to be swift and provide value to customers, but the adoption of the Agile manifesto changed the way IT departments work, enabling a greater level of agility in their operations. Although Agile was initially limited to software development, the Agile manifesto-driven concepts were later applied to form 'DevOps,' 'DevOpsSec,' etc. DevOps combines development and operations, working together to ensure smooth and seamless operations and hence, value delivery to the customers or consumers. Integrating Security with DevOps enables all three components to act swiftly to the changing dynamics in the internal and external world of IT.

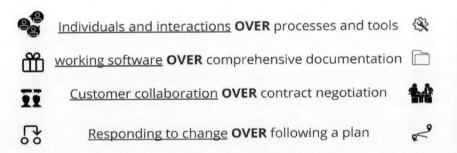

Figure 4 : Agile Manifesto

Although the Agile Manifesto looks simple, underneath it lies a powerful set of philosophical concepts. The manifesto has taken the IT industry very far in terms of speed, value, and delivery, hence the profitability of the IT department. While some companies have embraced the Agile manifesto as it is, others have adapted and extended the original. As a result, agility in the IT industry is higher compared to other industries or business units which do not follow similar concepts.

The Agile Manifesto has also helped to transform how people work. For example, IT practitioners who used to work individually in silos began to work as small teams with varying skills. They also started to learn other skill sets which improved their collaboration. This is how completely different skills such as 'user experience design' — which was developed using 'human-centric design'— were integrated into the IT industry. If you find a software engineer who can draw nice visuals or sketches, you should not be surprised. These professionals are constantly acquiring new skills to integrate into the IT process to enable them to improve their job performance.

Information technology continues to refine the process of creation for experts in the industry. Automation is one of the by-products of this refinement. If a task is repeated in the software development process, experts always find ways to automate it. For example, software testing has been automated. Pushing the code to production has been automated with a concept called 'CI-CD' or 'continuous integration and continuous deployment'. That means manual efforts have been reduced, and IT professionals can focus on more value-driven activities.

The result of all this is the advanced products end-users or consumers enjoy today. Information technology systems and products are now integrated into almost all the activities in our daily routines. In fact, without IT, our businesses would suffer massively.

Agile Success in IT

Research conducted by various institutes and individuals has proven that the right application of Agile has enabled the IT industry to be very successful. Standish Group, a global research organization, provides industry-leading research on software projects, covering more than 50,000 projects from different parts of the world.

According to the Standish Group's Chaos Report of 2015, the success rate of Agile-driven projects is high. As depicted in Table 1, Agile-driven projects have demonstrated a success rate that is three times higher than that of Waterfall-driven projects. From Standish Group's data sample, only 9% of Agile projects reported failures.

METHOD	SUCCESSFUL	CHALLENGED	FAILED
Agile	39%	52%	9%
Waterfall	11%	60%	29%

Table 2: Comparison: Agile Vs Waterfall
project successes (Standish Group, 2015)

In 2015, Serrador and Pinto et al. analyzed 1,386 projects to check for the success-failure ratio of Agile projects compared to non-Agile ones. .In that research, project success was measured differently from the traditional approach of cost, quality, and time. Serrador and Pinto went beyond those basic measurements and included the level of satisfaction of the following: sponsors and stakeholders, the project team, the client, the project or program manager, etc. .

Figure 5: Different ways to measure project success

The research revealed 6% of the 1,386 project samples studied were fully Agile, 65% of projects were partially Agile, and 32% of the projects did not have any Agile components. It demonstrated a correlation between the presence of iterative or Agile components in an IT project and its success rate. In those cases where Agile or iterative components were used, the projects were successful when measured by seven success criteria (see the diagram above). In addition, the research also found a correlation between the number of iterative components in a project and the project's success: When there were more iterative components in a project, the project's success increased. While academic research is scant in this area, this research provides some good insights that even now, not all projects in IT are Agile but those which use Agile components yield cost, time, and quality efficiencies and reach satisfying stakeholder project objectives.

Agile for Success: A Real Business Case

The M-company (not its real name), a not-for-profit, was one of the largest in the sector in the APAC region. More than 8,000 employees served millions of people, and it engaged more than 10,000 charities and donors for fundraising. Its IT service management software (ITSM) was 15 years old. Being a not-for-profit organization, they depended on money from charities, so they didn't spend much on their ITSM. But the system was slow, and it was time to sunset it. So, the CIO advised the board to invest in the latest cloud platform called 'Service Now'.

A consulting company was selected to implement the system. Nearly two million Australian dollars of investment was allocated, and the consulting company advised them they could get the system up and running in 12 months. The CIO led his internal team of 15 people and asked them to work with the consulting company.

The consulting company hand-held the M-company's project team. They created three folders with the requirement specification, solution design, and the contract. The documents were detailed enough, and the M-company program manager, the business owner, and the CIO were happy because now everything was documented, and they had something to refer back to.

Time ticked by. Every month the CIO, program manager, general manager, project manager, business owner, and consulting company got together for a steering committee of one hour. They went through a presentation that explained the program's status, which was looking very promising. At the end of the committee, they all went for lunch together, then the consulting company team went to their office in the south and M-company went to their office in the north.

Nine months passed. 1.6 million (AUD) was spent. In the next three months they expected to retire the old system and bring the new system to live. But something unexpected happened. Both the program manager and the senior business analyst who were leading the program resigned, creating a vacuum. While the recruitment was in progress, the CIO at the board meeting struggled to answer a series of questions from the board of directors. Would the system be delivered on time? Who would lead the program now? Would it go over budget? The questions remained unanswered. But everyone was clear that a miracle was needed.

With less than 100 days to go until the program deadline, I joined M-company. I had one mission: Rescue and deliver the program on time.

Within my first week on the job, I skimmed the three document folders but dumped them in a drawer. I talked to all the internal project team members. All of them were working on multiple projects. They had never interacted much with the consulting company team members apart from a once-a-week status update meeting and email communications. My next step was to talk to the M-company account director. I informed him that the consulting team should be co-located with M-company from the following week onward. He was initially hesitant, but I explained the risks of working in isolation and how the delays could mean possible termination of the contract, and he complied with my request.

The following week, the board room was converted into a war room. The M-company project team of 15 was relieved from other work and dedicated to the project for the next three months. Five members from the consulting company were stationed in the war room. We set up a Kanban board on one of the walls and gathered together an ample amount of post-it notes, sharpies, all sorts of stationery, lots of candy, and snacks. On the second day, I gave a crash course in Agile as iterative development, how to create a backlog of all the product features which needed to be developed, prioritizing mechanisms, sprint planning, stand-ups, showcase, etc.

All steering committee and status update meetings were abandoned. Instead, at the end of each week, the entire organization (if they wanted) would come to the board room to see the demonstration of the module the team had finished that week.

Then we kicked off the first sprint. It was a struggle at the beginning. Personalities clashed, but issues got resolved quickly, while egos started taking a back seat. They learned to understand each other and build empathy. The work they had in hand became the priority. When someone was struggling, another person jumped in to help because they had to get it done before Friday when the CIO, MD, and other senior stakeholders, as well as the entire organization, would come to see the working product at the showcase.

The waste reduced. There were no status update meetings or presentations to create, no context switching. They felt they were achieving a lot. They left for home at exactly 5:30 pm. When they came back the next day at 9:00 am, they had relaxed, slept well, and recharged their batteries by spending good quality time with their loved ones at home. The war room often resounded with laughter.

Exactly 96 days after they began this Agile way of working, M-company switched off their 15-year-old system and logged into the new ServiceNow system. All employees started using the system at the same time, and for nearly two months during the warranty period, there was not a single bug reported. The budget had gone over by just 2,190 Australian dollars. For a two-million-dollar program, 2,190 dollars was negligible.

The M-company started its Agile Center program after that, converting all projects to Agile and teaching everyone how to adopt it.

Summary

When applied in the right place and in the right manner, Agile is a magical tool, process, methodology, and culture that can deliver favorable results to all parties involved. It is difficult to find any IT company today that is not operating using Agile as a process and a methodology. Most software and product developments use the Agile way of working. As a result, they have gained mastery of the process and improved it by fixing any issues they have identified while using the methodology. For example, in the past, while software development was being done using Agile, IT operations were not being done in Agile, and both teams worked in isolation. This led to a new improvement you may have heard of as 'DevOps' (mentioned above), which is basically the Development and Operations departments working together. In addition, using Agile, IT teams have been able to identify work that could be automated.

The lesson to learn is that the Agile way of working significantly changed this development process. This drastic process and mindset change has benefited customers as well as the development team and as a result, when there is a catastrophe such as COVID-19, they are able to bounce back and adjust because their process is designed to accommodate changes and exploit the opportunities changes bring.

The Agile way of working is not only essential, but it is also a winning strategy, which is why many companies are now looking into applying Agile in areas of business where it has not been applied. But let's first understand what Agile consists of and build common ground on Agile understanding before we discuss its application in non-IT areas.

2

THE BUILDING BLOCKS OF AGILE

Many leaders are unfamiliar with Agile because it is a relatively new 'thing'. If you are a business leader with 20 years of experience, you were not taught anything called Agile when you were in business school. Even now, only a few universities and business schools teach Agile as a subject. Hence, it is not uncommon for leaders to know only a little about Agile. Such leaders will need to move quickly from 'know' Agile to 'do' Agile status as the Agile way of working is a game changer.

"Ask general managers what they know about Agile, and chances are they'll respond with an uneasy smile and a deflecting quip such as 'Just enough to be dangerous'. They may pepper conversations with terms like 'sprints' and 'time boxes' or use *agile* as an adjective to describe some new initiative and claim that their businesses are becoming more and more nimble. But because they haven't studied the methodology behind agile practices or seen agile teams in action, they couldn't really tell you what agile is all about or how it's actually working in their organization." (Rigby, HBR, 2020)

After working with a few companies who initiated Agile transformation in their workplaces, there are many reasons for me to agree with Darrell K. Rigby, a partner at Bain & Company, quoted above.

Increasingly, Agile is being injected into all organizations and business units. If you don't do it from the top, your team will do it from below. I did that in many organizations where I worked. When I saw a failing program, a delivery process with no value or a business unit struggling to be profitable, I changed the entire process or culture by moving into Agile which, in almost all cases, was eye-opening for the leaders to the point they wanted to adopt it.

Although I take pride in doing that, all Agile practitioners normally do the same because they know how good Agile is, so they start doing Agile without any initiatives from leadership. However, when the initiatives are taken by the C-level, the transformation is very powerful, and businesses can reap tremendous benefits. Hence, it is essential that leaders develop a good knowledge of Agile so that they can give leadership to such transformations.

Agile: Get to Know It Beyond the Basics

Agile is a subject area that is very easy to get lost in. To get a sense of what I mean, read through the paragraph below:

"Large scale scrum, scaled agile, release train engine, Agile portfolio canvas, Agile Center of Excellence, Kanban, Jira, version one, scrum master, chief product owner, CI/CD, test-driven development, feature-driven development, minimum viable

product (MVP), minimum marketable product, sprint, iteration, retrospective, showcase, continuous improvement, product owner, certified scrum master, extreme programming, pair programming, Agile coach, DevOps, DevSecOps, Agile maturity index, velocity, story points, Fibonacci numbers, WSJF, PI planning, area product owner, scrum of scrums, stand-ups, backlog grooming, backlog planning, backlog, sprint planning, continuous integration, continuous release, Agile values, manifesto, Agile ceremonies, enterprise agility, Agile organization".

Although these terms can sometimes be alienating, I am sure that you have heard many of these words in different places. While you might understand the meaning of some of them, they are just words with no meaning for the majority of people. It is understandable. The next section offers a simplified understanding of Agile for senior leaders.

Defining Agile

I always explain Agile as a **culture** and a **methodology**. It is a culture that facilitates the kind of environment needed to deliver value to customers, employees, and business partners. It is a culture that empowers employees — the people who have the most powerful tool: **knowledge**. It is a culture that encourages innovation by celebrating failures and a culture that inspires one to improve day by day. But this culture is hard to develop. Let me explain it by using the habit of smoking.

If you are a chain smoker who smokes 20 cigarettes a day, no matter what type of meeting you are in, you tend to take a break every half an hour or so for a smoke. You continue with this habit for a long time until your doctor shows you your black lungs and you get determined to stop the habit. The next day, you throw away your packets of cigarettes. However, in only a few hours, your body starts begging you for a cigarette and you feel frustrated not being able to fulfil this urge. In the end, you give in and pick up the habit again.

Implementing Agile works in a similar fashion. No matter how good the new habit is, you always have to fight against relapsing into the old ones, the old culture and the past way of working. Many people fall back into the old, toxic cultures as it is always hard to stay disciplined enough to keep the new habits.

Agile is a new culture. It brings a great deal of good and removes delays in various ways. The Agile Manifesto explains how.

The Origin of the Agile Manifesto

The birth of the Agile Manifesto dates back to 2001. Seventeen veterans of software development created the manifesto out of frustration with the process of traditional software development commonly known as Waterfall. Although originally developed for just software, the same principles can be applied to almost all types of products. In the next subsections, I explain the philosophies that serve as the building blocks of the Agile process.

Agile manifesto

 Individuals and interactions **OVER** processes and tools

 working software **OVER** comprehensive documentation

 Customer collaboration **OVER** contract negotiation

 Responding to change **OVER** following a plan

Individuals and interactions over processes and tools

All leaders are familiar with processes. Processes are designed to standardize work and bring some method to the madness. However, some processes do more harm than good. As an example, an organization I worked for had one of the longest employee recruitment cycles I have ever come across. When we wanted to recruit an employee in Australia, approval had to be given by an official working in the Netherlands. When asked why, the answer was simple, "It's the process." Some persisted, asking, "Why can't the decision-making be done by a leader in Australia if the position to be filled is in Australia?" The response from HR was always, "That's how it has been done for many years, so we cannot change the process."

In many cases, we have introduced processes and tools into our work that only add unnecessary waste. Some say it is SLAs; some say it is process. Processes should only be used when they are an absolute necessity. When the primary focus is value delivery, processes and tools may hinder that value delivery. Hence, when implementing processes and tools, we must first try to determine if a process will add value or if it will delay the delivery.

Working software over comprehensive documentation

Our workplaces often force us to produce massive amounts of documentation. The software development process has been no exception. In my previous example of the M-company, they had very nice documentation but no way to demonstrate working software for nine months. In most parts of a business, for example, leaders find it impossible to operate without PowerPoint presentations. The amount of time they spend creating presentations is staggering. If they spent the same time sitting and talking with everyone involved in the development, they would resolve the issues on the spot, making things much faster and more enjoyable.

Customer collaboration over contract negotiation

In most cases, product development involves at least two parties: the customer or client and a service provider, which is usually an IT consulting company. Throughout this process and even after that, the amount of time that goes into creating contracts is mind-blowing. The process is complicated and can be daunting as it involves lots of discussions relating to penalties, service level agreements, contractual obligations, non-disclosure agreements, etc. Some of these contractual processes can drag on for two, three months, and even up to six months.

The major reason for these long contractual processes is because each party is trying to protect itself should something go wrong. To do this, therefore, both parties seek to make sure that the contract items are very specific down to the tiniest details. Both parties consider what situations could arise at the various points on the product timeline if it is not delivered at the set time. This method is both disadvantageous and wasteful as it is built on suspicion rather than trust. Instead of this rigid process, what is needed is a flexible approach that caters to both parties and states what both must do to make the project successful. We need to cultivate trust and respect for the business model. This is where partnership is required instead of lengthy contracts.

Responding to change over following a plan

In the traditional way of working, creating plans to get things done is treated as important. Once created, following the plan is expected and any deviations require changes to the contractual terms and lengthy discussions. This result is that changes are less welcome. But changes will always come and there is no way to predict what they might be. The COVID-19 global pandemic is a perfect example. Did anybody predict the pandemic or plan to work the way we did over the last years?

If your main revenue stream is from your customers, it doesn't matter if you have the best processes in place if the customers are not happy. And one way to make customers happy is to have a receptive attitude towards changes because customers do change their mind, all the time.

Hence, if businesses are focusing on customer experience, customer value delivery, and making a sustainable business model, it is essential to build a culture where changes are welcomed and accommodated.

Agile Practices

Agile practices have been implemented over and over again with consistent results, indicating this is the best way forward. Most Agile practices are applicable as they are. For example, daily team catch-ups called 'stand-ups' were used even before they were labeled as an Agile practice. Empirical studies show that these practices are effective when practiced regularly. Below are a few of these Agile practices in detail.

Small teams

Agile teams comprise small numbers, usually around three to nine, with 11 as the maximum. Agile practitioners are adamant about this practice. Having three to nine members in a team allows effective organization and reduces delays due to communication gaps (which can lead to misunderstandings and chaos). This point is illustrated in the figure below.

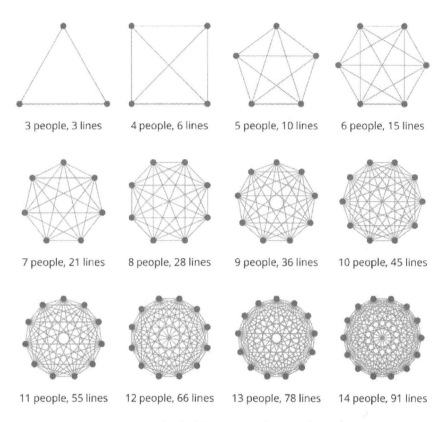

3 people, 3 lines   4 people, 6 lines   5 people, 10 lines   6 people, 15 lines

7 people, 21 lines   8 people, 28 lines   9 people, 36 lines   10 people, 45 lines

11 people, 55 lines   12 people, 66 lines   13 people, 78 lines   14 people, 91 lines

Figure 6: The link between the number of
people and the communication channels

Larger teams require more communication, and the technological complexity that results slows the development pace (Carlson and Turner, 2013). If you work in an organization with thousands of staff members, getting everyone on the same page will be very difficult. Therefore, Agile teams are small and are thus able to respond quickly to any changing situation. With a small team, communication is much more effective and swifter, allowing faster response and reaction times.

Multidisciplinary teams

An ideal Agile team is cross-functional and self-sufficient in terms of skill sets. This represents an enterprise in a miniature version. Like at the executive level, where strategic leadership consists of finance, supply chain, operations, HR, IT leaders, etc., there should be cross-functional representation at team level, too. In the context of software development, an Agile team will consist of UX (user experience) designers, business analysts, software engineers, IT infrastructure designers, and developers. When people with these different skills are brought together to form a team, they become a self-sufficient unit that can respond to any changes originating from the customer instantly, without depending on another unit. This makes the process faster and better.

Co-located teams

Agile teams are co-located. The team shares one workspace rather than being scattered across various locations. As they are physically located in one place, they do not have to write emails or set up meetings to communicate with one another. Setting up meetings can be time-consuming. Doing some simple math, if it takes ten minutes to schedule a meeting, it will take one hour to schedule six meetings. The process of doing this is long because the right people have to be in attendance, a meeting room secured, an agenda prepared, etc.

Working in a co-located space simplifies this process and even encourages face-to-face communication. This also helps to foster bonding, respect, and appreciation among the team members. No one is perfect, and sometimes there will be friction. If they have a problem with a team member's behavior, they discuss it and find a middle ground to live with it. Because the team is co-located, they will always find a way to complement each other's good behaviors.

Dedicated teams

In 2009, a Stanford professor, Clifford Nass, did research with 262 students. He assumed multitaskers achieve a lot because they can do many things in the same time frame. He set up two groups, multitaskers and non-multitaskers. Then he analyzed each group's outcome in various activities. The results were that multitaskers are literally lousy at everything they do. The rationale goes back to the effort it takes to regain focus when context switching. Context switching wastes a lot of time in terms of getting your attention back on the job at hand.

I have put this into practice in many formats, in both my personal and professional life. In my professional life, I have set up projects with people dedicated to one project and people dedicated to multiple projects at the same time. In almost all cases, when I had team members working on multiple projects simultaneously, all the projects they were working on got delayed, resulting in budget overrun. On the other hand, when the teams were working only on one project, they finished the work even before the deadline, gaining significant cost savings for the customer. This was also the case for the service-providing companies, as they could finish the projects earlier and take up another project, hence increasing the portfolio and revenue.

Include the customer in the team

Delivering value to the customers is one of the hardest jobs because customers have different expectations that can sometimes keep changing. It is difficult to understand what the customer really needs and often even customers cannot explain that properly! Henry Ford has said if he had asked customers what they wanted, they would have said they needed a faster horse.

No matter how difficult it is to understand what the customer values, if they do not get what they need, they will not stay your customer for long. Hence, it is important to try to understand and figure out what the customer really needs. In order to do this, the gaps between the customer and the teams who develop the value for the customer need to be reduced.

Most of the time, from the company's perspective, customers are distant entities involved only at the beginning and end of the product development process. This issue can be resolved by co-creating the product with the customer. For example, when we create software products, we always make the customers a part of the Agile team, either as a product owner or a business analyst. Every time we have co-created with the customers by directly integrating them into the teams, the products, projects, and solutions have been successful, and they gained returns on their investments.

Planning incrementally and delivering continuously

If you were to plan what you are going to do at 11 am on December 26th next year, that would be a pointless exercise. But you *can* plan what you are going to do at 11 am tomorrow effortlessly and with a much greater level of accuracy.

The concept of planning one step at a time is integrated into Agile through the principle of incremental planning. Under this practice, the level of planning adopted is that which is just enough to get the work done and prevent waste in the planning exercises. Agile incorporates a few levels of planning, but the level of detail involved is dependent on the time and the framework. For example, Agile teams plan their work at the beginning of every iteration, say, fortnightly. Planning is done as a collective effort with a 360-degree view in order to greatly reduce the chances of failure. The details that go into the planning are just enough so that the team understands their commitments.

During the iteration planning, the team does not discuss what they are going to do on a Friday, for example. Instead, when Friday comes, they plan what is to be done in the morning of that day. Because of the shorter time frame in view, it is easier for the team to plan their day more accurately and also achieve set objectives for that period.

Once a team achieves its set objectives after a couple of iterations, the members become very confident and much more accurate with the planning process. This makes the team prepared and up to the task, therefore less likely to fail in delivering on its commitments to the customers. This way, customers get what they need continuously without failure. On the other hand, the team is satisfied and does not needlessly expend efforts that go to waste.

Flat structure of Agile teams

Agile teams have no hierarchies, with all team members in an equal position. This structure drives them to unleash their potential. When there are hierarchies and managers telling team members what to do and how to do it, they begin to work based on the manager's knowledge and experience rather than on team members' thinking capabilities. The result is that team members will never develop the confidence to tap into their own capabilities, leadership, experience, and knowledge. It creates followers rather than leaders. It also adds delays as team members have to wait until they are given orders by the leaders up the hierarchy.

In the workplaces of the future, it will be important that every team member or employee is able to become a leader rather than merely a follower. As a business leader, just imagine how much time could be saved if all employees were able to make business decisions just like you. It is, therefore, important that employees work based on their capacity and knowledge. In some cases, employees may know a lot more than their managers or it may be the other way around.

Today, most workplaces are built on the idea that managers are supposed to always tell the employees what to do. I was once in a project meeting where one of the project managers told a team member that he had to build a web page in two days. The team member, a very talented software engineer who was always thorough in his work, tried to explain to the project manager that the task could not be done in two days because it was a complicated assignment. But the project manager countered that he used to do such web development and he challenged it could be done in two hours. That was a humiliating comment for the software engineer. He walked up to the project manager and placed his laptop in front of the manager, saying, "Okay, please show me how to do that in two hours. I'd love to know how a web page that should take five days to complete could be done in two hours."

Everyone in the meeting watched on with amusement, and the project manager quickly changed the subject. Not only that, the software engineer resigned within two weeks, and the project manager struggled to hire a software engineer for the next four months. The results could have been very different if the project manager had enough faith in the software engineer that he required more than two days to complete the work because that was his capability. The project manager might have had a different skill set and experience, hence he could have done the job in two hours, but that does not mean everyone else was of his caliber.

The essence of sharing this experience is to point out that there needs to be respect for each team member's knowledge, capabilities, and experience. Not having hierarchies means that team members trust each other to give their best to their defined tasks. Such non-hierarchical structures motivate them to help each other and finish the work they have committed to as a team. When managers have to instruct, saying "you do this", "you do that", "you help him" etc., it is hard to foster a collective work mindset. It is also not the best way to use a manager's time and expertise.

Transparency of work

When we talk about how Agile helps businesses to be productive, effective, and reduce waste, transparency of work comes into the picture. The adoption of practices like visual workflows (e.g., using Kanban walls: Figure 7) and daily stand-ups helps to make the work visible to everyone. Hence, everyone in the team (including the customers) is on the same page in terms of what is to be done, when, and how.

If any team member is falling behind, it is discussed, and help is offered to ensure that the work is completed as planned and committed to by all.

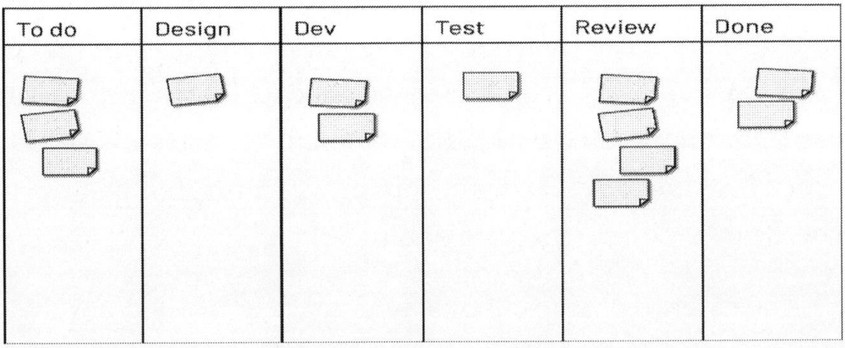

To do	Design	Dev	Test	Review	Done

Figure 7 : Visual Kanban wall

Continuous feedback and improvements

One key practice that allows Agile teams to thrive is the practice of continuous improvement. That means they continuously look back at the process they followed and assess it critically, and if it worked, they decide together to continue the process. But if it did not work, then they make decisions to change it. And they do this at regular intervals, mostly at every iteration.

At the end of each iteration or sprint, the team members sit down together to discuss what went wrong, what went right, and what needs improvement. This discussion is usually very constructive as there is no passing judgment or issuing of punishment for failure. Because of this approach, iteration by iteration, the Agile team improves its performance as they start operating like a small business that produces profit, month after month.

Figure 8 : The normal culture of resisting continuous improvement

This session is strictly restricted to team members. There are no managers or anyone outside the team present. As a result, the session is open, honest, and constructive as every individual gives feedback on how and what needs improvement. Then, based on the analysis and feedback given, the team decides what corrective actions are required and takes ownership of implementing these actions from the next iteration onwards. In addition, they agree to continue doing what was working. This practice alone adds a huge productivity bump to the team's workflow and resembles the 'lean' practices illustrated in the figure ...

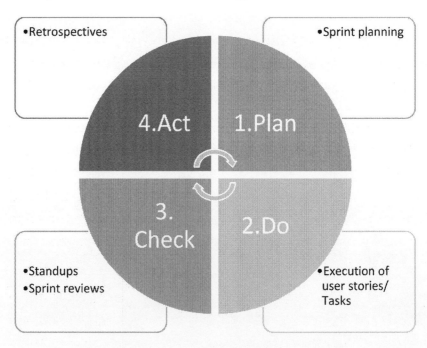

Figure 9 : Plan, do, check, adjust cycle of lean

Maintain an optimal workload

Gmail was not a product Google leaders asked their employees to create. The platform started as a fun project put together by a few like-minded people. It was part of Google's policy that encourages innovation among its employees. In Google, employees can allocate 20% of their normal workweek towards a fun product. They can collaborate with anyone in the company for the project, and managers or leaders do not need to know about it. One of the results of this policy is Gmail, one of Google's top products and also one of their main revenue-generators.

It is this kind of policy business leaders should consider adopting. Happy employees mean a happy business that generates happy customers. Happy employees do not leave their employers even when competitors offer them better options. This saves the intellectual property of the company plus the costs associated with conducting a new hiring exercise. This kind of policy increases employee satisfaction and retention rates. Also, satisfied employees become brand ambassadors for their company, propagating its products and services outside the office environment. This helps to reduce reputational damage and increase brand awareness.

Agile teams do this using the lean principle of 'pulling work'. This means that each team decides the capacity of their team for an iteration, and based on this agreed capacity, 'pull' from their prioritized set of work that matches their optimal capacity. This way, they are able to finish the work by the agreed date and take on a new task. Working on a task or project, one at a time, allows team members to concentrate their energy on one part to finish it without defects.

This approach also gives the team the time and breathing space needed to think and work. Employees need to exercise, socialize, build working relationships, learn new things, and create innovative products. The optimal flow and pull system adopted by Agile teams empowers employees to enjoy their work while being passionate about it instead of just working like machines. When employees have enough time to 'think and work' rather than 'just work', they always produce amazing results.

Daily stand-ups

One of the most impactful, effective, and productive Agile practices every Agile team uses is the 'daily stand-up'. When done correctly, this simple practice spurs massive change, from a better work culture and ethics to the quality of effort put in the production or development process.

All team members meet daily for 15 minutes at a designated place, usually in front of the Kanban wall. Regardless of the location, this meeting must happen at the predetermined place and time. The meeting must always start on time and finish on time: that is, it should not exceed 15 minutes. During this time, each team member gives an update on their work. Everyone formalizes their update by answering three simple questions:

- What did I plan and complete yesterday?
- What am I going to complete today?
- What is blocking my work?

For example, a software engineer might give an update like this:

"Yesterday, I developed the home page of the website as planned. Today, I will complete the testing of the home page on all three devices — Windows laptop, Apple iPhone and Android phone. I am all good to complete the work today, but I need an Android phone. Can someone lend me an Android phone, so I won't be blocked?"

This simple update is more than enough for the team and the leaders to understand that the home page will be completed by the end of the day if the developer gets access to an Android phone. So, someone from the team will lend him an Android phone and if no one has one, then the leaders will take the necessary action to secure one so that he can finish the work as planned.

The information contained in this update is enough for the team members to assess if they are moving forward as a team or if they are going to be stuck at roadblocks. If the latter is the case, then they will have to discuss with the leaders how to remove the obstacles. The daily stand-ups do not include any PowerPoint or status update report presentations; just 15 minutes of updating, which is more than enough for everybody to get up to speed with the latest developments.

This daily session is time boxed. That means it always stays within the time frame and good Agile coaches know how to get the teams to adopt this time boxed approach. This simple practice can add big improvements to any Agile teams, business units and organizations.

The effect of this stand-up is multifold. I have seen chief operating officers attending daily stand-ups of critical products/projects. By just being present at the stand-up meetings, they got to know the project's status and product development that day. It allowed them to get the operational details required to make their strategic decisions without needing to schedule specific status update meetings with teams. They obtained all the information they wanted by monitoring the Kanban wall and attending the stand-ups, so they did not need to disturb the teams in their work.

Agile Frameworks

Agile frameworks are blueprints developed by Agile practitioners after years and years of practical experimenting to get the right balance of structure, process, people, and culture. Some practitioners have established institutions around these frameworks, such as 'Scrum Alliance', 'Scrum. Org', or 'Scaled Agile'. Some are profit-based, while some are not-for-profit, and they are interested in advocating for others to adopt the frameworks so the wider communities and businesses can benefit from them.

Some Agile frameworks are simple and can be adopted without much effort, while others are complicated and require incredibly good professional guidance and coaching for adoption. For example, the Scaled Agile Framework is complicated and developed for specific purposes, as discussed below. Proper guidance is needed to implement a framework like this. As a leader, you need to have some knowledge of each of these frameworks to determine how much expert guidance is necessary. However, if you are a Chief Agile Officer, a mastery of all is essential.

Different Agile frameworks

Below is a list of Agile frameworks that are popular among various organizations:

- Scrum
- Kanban
- Scrumban
- Disciplined Agile 2.0
- Dynamic Systems Development Method (DSDM), now referred to as Framework for Business Agility
- Enterprise Scrum
- Large-Scale Scrum (LeSS)
- Nexus
- Recipes for Agile Governance in the Enterprise (RAGE)
- Scaled Agile Framework (SAFe)
- Scaled Agile Lean Development (ScALeD)
- Scrum at Scale
- Spotify
- eXponential Simple Continuous Autonomous Learning Ecosystem (XSCALE)

Frameworks like Scrum, Large-Scale Scrum, Spotify, Kanban, Nexus, and the Scaled Agile Framework are used more frequently compared to others and they have very specific applications. Some of the common agile frameworks are explained in the next section.

Scrum Framework

According to *The Scrum Guide*, Scrum is a simple framework for effective team collaboration on complex software projects (www.Scrum.org, 2018). Most Agile professionals entered the Agile world after studying or practicing Scrum as a framework. This framework was created for IT software development. However, the concept behind the Scrum framework is applicable to many other industries. It has even been applied in the very unconventional area of the oil and gas sector — more on that later. For now, suffice to say that the Scrum framework is a simple but very powerful tool.

How does the Scrum framework work?

The Scrum is the simplest and most widely used framework. Built upon the Agile Manifesto and principles, it follows a flat structure, with very simple roles and practices called 'ceremonies'.

The scrum team, known as a 'development team', consists of seven to nine cross-functional team members. The scrum team is divided into three roles, the scrum master, the product owner, and the Agile team. The number of team members are fixed and does not change over a period. The team takes the ownership of developing a product or a service and delivers value to the customer in an incremental manner. In that way, customers are provided with continuous value from the very beginning without a longer waiting time like in Waterfall structures. These increments are usually called sprints, which can be one, two, three or four weeks long.

The product owner, with the consultation of the customer, creates a product backlog that consists of different requirements identified as epics, features, or user stories. The work is prioritized based on the value and how urgent it is for the customer, then the team pulls the work from the prioritized list. At the end of the sprint, they produce a working product whose features can be consumed or enjoyed by the customers.

The team uses different practices like daily stand-ups, iterative development, sprint planning, retrospectives and sprint showcases.

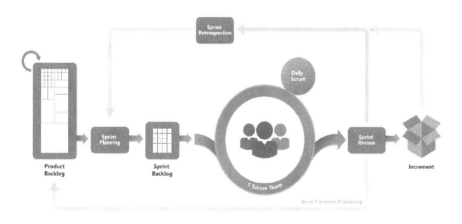

Figure 10: Scrum framework (Scrum.org)

Nexus Agile Framework

Nexus Agile framework is a Scrum-based large-scale framework designed for product development. It was founded by Ken Schwaber, who is also one of the founders of the Agile Manifesto. The way Nexus works can be explained with the following analogy.

Let's assume there is a need for a three-bedroom house, and you assemble a small multi-disciplinary team of eight members to build the house in one month. This means that at the end of one month, a family can move into the house. On the other hand, let's also assume you get a contract to build a ten-unit housing complex. If you use the same eight-person team, then it will take ten months to complete the project. However, if you decided to create a similar eight-person team to handle each unit of the housing complex, that is, ten different eight-person teams, it means that ten housing units will be ready at the end of one month and ten families can move in. This is what the Nexus framework does to the software development process.

However, the process is not as easy as it has just been explained. In the real process, complexities can arise. So, the development process requires effective coordination, synchronization, and orchestration. Everybody must move at the same speed, style, and rhythm, like a marching army. The process has to be guided. The Nexus framework builds a set of principles, activities, and structures to provide this synchronization.

When can Nexus be applied?

Nexus can be used for large product development that needs hundreds of people structured around a few small teams. It may not be applicable for developing a small mobile app or a product like a website. However, if the product is a complex one with many integrations with third parties or features in the product itself, then Nexus will be ideal. For example, let's assume a Customer Relationship Management (CRM) product is needed. If the product needs a mobile application, iOS and Android versions, in addition to a web application and other features for sales, marketing and customer support, then it will be ideal to adopt the Nexus framework for this product.

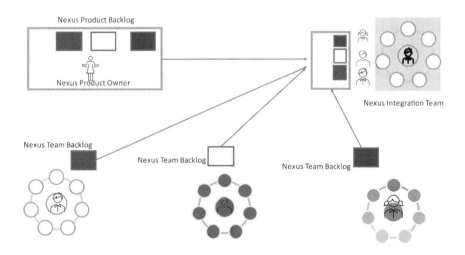

Figure 11 : Nexus product development process

The foundation of Nexus

The Nexus Guide defines the Nexus Agile framework as "a group of approximately three to nine Scrum Teams that work together to deliver a single product; it is a connection between people and things". Nexus preserves the scrum team's power while also extending it into a powerful integration of multiple scrum teams. The number of teams integrated always ranges between three to nine and one of the teams is a special team designated the 'Nexus Integration Team'.

The Nexus Integration Team

The Nexus Integration Team (NIT), which comprises seven to nine members, operates on Scrum principles and practices and integrates various tasks executed by individual scrum teams into developing a final product. The best way I can explain NIT is by using a kinetic rain artwork. Before you read the next section, just do a YouTube search of the text, 'Art at Changi: Kinetic Rain.'

Figure 12: The Kinetic rain at Changi Airport- Singapore

Kinetic rain is an artwork that uses precise synchronization of metallic pieces representing raindrops. The sculpture consists of 608 copper-plated aluminum raindrops. These drops are connected by steel wires to computer-controlled motors that raise and lower them with precision level coordination. The smooth movement is then aligned to selected music. Whatever the music, the raindrops dance to it. The smooth synchronization of these 608 individual pieces is mesmerizing and addicting, powerful enough to make one forget that they are in the middle of a busy airport in Singapore.

If we use this artwork as an analogy to explain how Nexus works, then each copper raindrop represents each scrum team. That is 608 scrum teams. The music composition resembles another scrum team, while the computer-controlled motors could be another scrum team that produces computer programs to control the movement of the scrum teams. The NIT is the team that controls the integration of all these teams and makes it move smoothly as one unit. As you can imagine, this integration team is just as important as the scrum team, as the final product depends on how individual outcomes are integrated.

The members of the NIT are the product owner, the scrum master and other integration team members. These integration team members are dedicated members of the integration team. However, situations might arise where integration members can come from other scrum teams as well. This means it is possible for an integration team member to be 75% dedicated to the NIT with 25% commitment to their scrum team (the percentage is context-driven). In cases where the product is complex and integration efforts are high, all members may be fully committed to the NIT.

The NIT teams hold daily stand-ups with representatives from the scrum teams in attendance. There are updates on issues relating to dependencies, and other risks that emerge from the process are highlighted to be resolved. The NIT makes sure continuous integration is done, tested, and communicated back to the scrum teams.

At the end of each sprint, the NIT conducts a sprint review in collaboration with the scrum teams and showcases the result to the stakeholders and customers. It is important to note that there is no separate scrum-level showcase as the final work is the integrated work. Also, the NIT conducts a retrospective assessment to improve the whole process continuously.

Nexus product backlog

A Nexus framework has a single product owner who manages a single product backlog from which the scrum teams work. The product owner decides the priority of the product items in line with the priorities highlighted by the customer. The product backlog items are broken down into smaller components that fit into one sprint. Later, at a sprint planning session, each team picks the product features/user stories/items from the main product backlog and takes that to the respective team to implement it in the sprint.

Nexus sprint planning

Sprint planning happens at the beginning of the sprint just like in the Scrum framework. Representatives from each scrum team and the NIT meet with the product owner at the start of the sprint. The product owner then clarifies the sprint goals based on the priorities identified to be aligned with the product goal. This sprint goal is a subset of the product goal and must be accomplished by the end of the sprint by all the scrum teams. Once the details are discussed, questions answered and dependencies mentioned, a possible solution is identified. After this, an agreement on what is to be done in each sprint is reached. This is then followed by commitments to the sprint goal by the teams. After this process, the selected user story/feature is then taken to the individual scrum team for further deconstruction to fit the team and to begin the work.

Nexus product owner (NPO)

The Nexus product owner is the sole custodian of the product. The NPO works with the customer and the stakeholder to understand what is needed and develop the product. The NPO, the NIT and representatives of the scrum teams develop the product backlog as prioritized.

Large-Scale Scrum (LeSS) Framework

Unlike small start-ups, most organizations have many employees and need multiple teams working together to produce a given piece of work or product. For example, let's assume you want to operate the entire HR business function using Agile. If the organization is large and has many HR professionals responsible for different HR functions, then just one scrum team may not be enough to execute the task. It might, therefore, be necessary to scale up the project to meet scaled-up requirements. In this kind of situation, the LeSS is a good framework to adopt.

LeSS helps to develop larger solutions using the Scrum framework. It applies Agile across multiple scrum teams. The number of scrum teams can be two or eight or even more (that is, more than 50 team members collectively). All teams have a single master product backlog which maintains the unified vision of the product and is the source for all the teams. However, when it comes to planning the sprint, each team selects a prioritized product feature from the master backlog to add to the team's backlog. The product features developed by multiple teams will then be integrated into one at the end of each sprint. Therefore, a large product feature can be developed and shipped in a significantly shorter period of two weeks or so.

There are additional practices to coordinate multiple teams such as creating the master product backlog and integrations, in addition to practicing Scrum at the team level. Imagine if your Salesforce CRM implementation or Human Resource Department's operations were done using a LeSS framework; there are faster and better results if leaders operate using this framework.

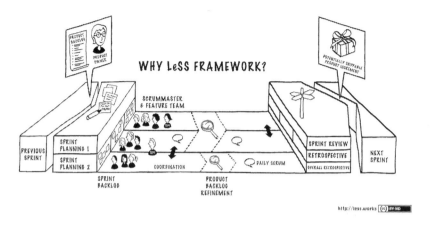

Figure 13 : LeSS Framework (Less.works)

Kanban

Kanban is the easiest to implement and is the simplest workflow management system. It can be used in any team and environment to operationalize the daily work or BAU functions. It operates using the pull system philosophy.

The team pulls the work from the queue to the workflow, finishes it off and then pulls the next piece of work. Therefore, the work is always transparent and team members always work on one piece of work at a time without losing focus due to huge demands. If you go to a bank, the customer service center operations are probably done using a Kanban system. At the entrance, you will be given a token and the current queue length will be displayed on a screen (transparency). When an operator pulls the next customer to their workflow, a call is made for the relevant token, and this is immediately updated on the screen showing the progress of the queue.

This method is also a good indicator for senior managers of the maximum load at present, allowing them to allocate resources accordingly to maintain a smooth flow. As an example, if there are more customers and the queue length is increasing, then the person operating the flow or in charge may decide to open a few more service desks so that the queue length can be reduced. This allows a maximum work in progress or WIP, which is a common Kanban rule limiting how many customers they can serve at a time to maintain optimal work progress. Hence, this reduces chaos due to multitasking and creates a smooth input and output flow.

Scaled Agile Framework (SAFe)

The Scaled Agile Framework (SAFe) connects all the layers of an organization. It links strategy to the portfolio levels, the portfolio levels to the solutions and the solutions to the program levels. The program levels are then connected to the team level using Agile principles and practices. SAFe is a great way of running each layer of an enterprise using Agile concepts. It is a bit complex, but if applied correctly, it can scale Agile across the enterprise.

In my experience, SAFe is the most successful framework in the corporate world. Under this process, several hundreds of people, sometimes even thousands, are working toward a common goal with the same passion. This is not to say that SAFe is perfect. In fact, it is always evolving.

The implementation of SAFe has been made easier with a clear roadmap, which starts from the leadership layer.

Most organizations fail in their adoption of Agile because their leadership styles do not align with Agile values and principles. When we implement Agile, we see that teams do quickly adapt to it, but management does not. This means that the organization cannot reap the full benefits expected from such a transformation. For this reason, SAFe starts from the leadership team and trains them on adopting the Agile mindset, principles, and practices. This sequence helps to build the right environment for the Agile teams by enabling them to be fully autonomous.

Spotify

Apple and Spotify have revolutionized the music industry. Apple introduced the iPod which stores thousands of songs, thereby changing the way we enjoy music. Before that, we used portable music players that could store only a few songs. Spotify, on the other hand, offers streaming as a service to its millions of subscribers. Unlike Apple, Spotify is device-independent and available on almost any platform as long as there is an internet connection. In fact, higher subscription packages allow users to store their music playlist offline.

From 2006 to 2018, Spotify grew to have 3,000 employees. Today, it has about 170 million users, 75 million of them being paying customers. In 2017, the company generated €4.09 billion in revenue (Wikipedia.org, 2019). This is significant growth for a new business model that was unique at the time the company was established. How did Spotify achieve this success? Among the many factors that contributed to its meteoric rise, such as leadership and a new business model, their product development framework deserves credit. They call this framework 'Spotify'.

The Spotify model

Spotify has a unique, flat organizational structure with minimal hierarchies. These small teams or 'squads' are empowered to be autonomous and self-sufficient with cross-functional skills. Spotify is structured based on squads, tribes, chapters, and guilds. Let's examine this model in more detail because this framework fits most of the business units that need to operate in an Agile way.

Squads

The squad is like the scrum team. It works like a mini start-up and runs like a business. They are self-sufficient in terms of resources, and they make their own decisions on how to run their own business.

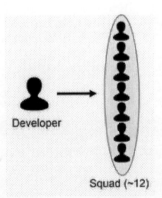

Figure 14: Squad

A squad consists of six to 12 members that comprise the UX designers, researchers, developers, testers, and other experts. All have equal rights and hold an equal position in terms of hierarchy. A squad has a flat hierarchy, and its leader is a servant leader who uses a skill set like that of a scrum master. This means that the leader facilitates stand-ups and showcase exercises, helps the product owner to refine the product backlog and coaches or assists the team in getting their impediments resolved. The team decides how to operate, whether to use Scrum or Kanban or extreme programming. The team members make decisions and take responsibility for successes or failures.

Tribes

Squads are grouped based on a theme and these groupings are known as tribes. A tribe can have a few squads (maybe five to seven or more) and is structured mostly on the basis of the product they are building.

A tribe can also be based on a solution the group is tasked with building. For example, all CRM squads form a CRM tribe, and each squad of the CRM tribe develops and releases a different feature of the final product, the CRM. The features relevant to sales are done by the 'sales squad,' while those that are relevant to marketing are done by the 'marketing squad'.

A tribe has a 'tribe leader,' and this person is usually an experienced 'squad leader' who has had the opportunity to work in one or more squads.

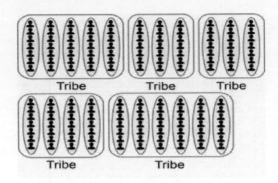

Figure 15: Tribes (Henrik Kniberg & Anders Ivarsson, 2012)

Chapters

A chapter consists of members with similar interests or skill sets. For example, a product owner's chapter is different from that of a UX designers. It is similar to a community of practice (CoP).

Chapters allow individuals to grow their knowledge and skills in their specific areas of practice. They may conduct training to share best practices or other activities.

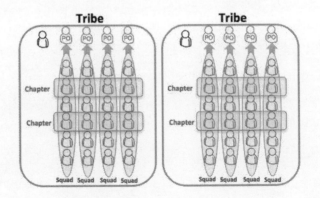

Figure 16: Tribes (Henrik Kniberg & Anders Ivarsson, 2012)

Guilds

A guild is a community of interest. People who want to share their interests and knowledge from different tribes can form guilds. It does not necessarily target individuals who have a particular skill set; a guild could be made up of people who just wish to learn. For instance, a guild for 'public speaking' can be created and anyone who wants to participate can be a member. This is an alternative way to upskill people in different disciplines.

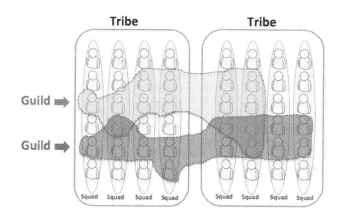

Figure 17 : Guilds (Henrik Kniberg & Anders Ivarsson, 2012)

The Spotify model gained popularity during attempts to implement Agile across various business units. In my experience with this framework, it shows promising results within a business environment. For example, this model has been applied with some twists to a banking environment consisting of IT, sales, customer service, marketing, HR, finance, and corporate risk management departments.

The implementation of this model for a major bank, whose transformation plan covered over 300 people, was aided by ten different Agile transformation consultants. The process seemed like putting in place a new organizational structure — and in a way, it was. The implementation did not only change the way the staff members operated, but it also delivered excellent results, particularly by preventing business units from acting in isolation. Many organizations are beginning to adopt this framework for their businesses. For example, some pharmaceutical companies like Roche are aggressively implementing the Spotify model to gain business agility.

However, these Agile frameworks only serve as a foundation or blueprint. To apply any of them to one's business, one needs to carefully select the right framework for the right place. A wrong selection can deliver unexpected negative results. Hence, the guidance of an Agile expert is indispensable.

Agile Roles

In the Agile world, there are a few roles with distinct responsibilities. The names of these roles may differ, and names are sometimes used interchangeably. Some roles are specific to some Agile frameworks.

Scrum master

Figure 18: Agile Team

The scrum master is the steward of the Agile process, playing a key role in the team but with a servant-leadership position. They carry a wealth of theoretical and practical knowledge about the Agile process and can guide the team and the product owner in the right direction in terms of Agile practices. They are also teachers or coaches, helping others, including teams and product owners, to navigate tough situations. The scrum master coaches and guides the product owner on the product development process, such as how to create the product backlog and how the features should be prioritized. If the team, including the product owner, is new to Agile, the scrum master can train them on Agile.

Scrum masters are servant leaders quite different to project managers. While serving the internal scrum team, scrum masters also connect with the external teams and leaders to find solutions to issues the team has highlighted as 'blockers' or 'impediments'. Scrum masters possess very good leadership qualities and avoid the 'command-and-control' way of doing things, but they are also very smart at leading the team to their destination. There are many scrum masters, but there are only a few great scrum masters.

A trap to avoid is assigning a project manager to the role of scrum master. Not that project managers cannot be great scrum masters, but project managers usually exhibit authoritative, command-and-control leadership, which is the opposite of the servant leadership required by a scrum master. However, with good coaching and mentoring, one can become a great scrum master.

Chief scrum master

The scrum master serves one Agile team. But often larger programs or teams across multiple business units need to come together to deliver a program or a larger product. Imagine the construction of a housing complex. Multiple teams need to work together simultaneously to deliver such massive scale products. And all teams need synchronization and orchestration using Agile practices. The chief scrum master does that orchestration and often works with multiple scrum masters who represent different Agile teams.

A scrum master who has extremely good leadership skills and years of experience with Agile mastery is a perfect candidate for such a role.

Release train engineer

The release train engineer or RTE is specific to certain frameworks like SAFe. In fact, as I understand it, the term was coined by the SAFe. Release train engineers lead a program using SAFe practices. The RTE resembles a program manager in the traditional world, synchronizing multiple projects to deliver the work of a program. But in the Agile world, SAFe is used as the framework for the job of the RTE. The RTE provides SAFe leadership for about ten teams or nearly 150 team members. RTEs will organize Agile release trains or programs, execute program planning called program increment or PI in every quarter, take the ownership of delivering the PIs and work with the leadership team to develop KPIs and measure the success or the failure of the program work. Some RTEs can be accountable for delivering million-dollar program work.

Agile team

An Agile team is the third pillar of the Agile team (the other two pillars are the scrum master and the product owner). The Agile team consists of cross-functional team members. Agile teams live and breathe Agile values like customer focus, customer collaboration, value delivery, minimizing delays and self-organization. They operate using Agile practices like daily stand-ups, time boxing, retrospectives, and product showcases.

They work with the scrum master and product owner collaboratively and constantly look into improving the processes they follow. These teams are interchangeably called squads, pods or scrum teams. With the scrum master and product owner, the team is one functional unit with the power and capabilities to develop and deliver a product or service.

Product owner

Product owner is one of the most important roles in Agile. The product owner is often the voice of the customer and focuses on what adds value to them. The product owner is authorized to make decisions on what features need to be added to the product or service and how to prioritize. The product owner needs a 360-degree view of the product starting from product vision to product delivery.

The product owner's main responsibility is to make sound decisions collectively on the product features, value creation, and prioritization of the delivery. Deciding what features should be delivered first and why is aligned with the product vision and is an important part of the product owner's job.

According to the Scrum framework, the responsibilities of a product owner are as below.

- Clearly express product backlog items.
- Order the items in the product backlog to best achieve goals and missions.
- Optimize the value of the work the development team performs.
- Ensure that the product backlog is visible, transparent, and clear to all, and shows what the scrum team will work on next.
- Ensure the development team understands items in the product backlog to the level needed.

The Scrum framework also mention the attributes a product owner should have as the following.

- Empowered. Has decision-making authority for the product.
- Business-savvy. Knows the business, the customer, and the market.
- Persuasive. Able to work well with the team and the stakeholders.
- Knowledgeable. Knows the market and the product. Grasps production challenges.
- Available: Is readily accessible to the team and to the stakeholders.

(ScrumAlliance.org, 2020)

Agile coach

Unlike Scrum masters or product owners, Agile coaches are not constant members of the team. The role of an Agile coach is to guide and facilitate. From time to time, Agile coaches use different methodologies to help the teams do better. At the very beginning, if the teams are very new, the Agile coach will play a teacher, trainer, and doer role. The coach will teach the Agile way of working to the team and sometimes deliver full training on certain frameworks. Then the coach will guide the team on a daily basis until they are very familiar with the Agile practices and mature in the Agile way of working. The Agile coach will facilitate Agile ceremonies like sprint planning, daily stand-ups, retrospectives, product showcases, etc. They also help with strategic areas such as selecting the right products, services to be done in Agile, framework selection, tools selection, process set up and cadence development.

Once the team is matured, then Agile coaches work on how to improve the team to move from the stage where they are to a high-performing level. This way of coaching is normally known as the 'Shu Ha Ri' method. At the very beginning, the team follows the Agile coach step by step. The team will simply do what the Agile coach says because they are very new to Agile and need to learn. That is the 'Shu' stage. But in the second stage of 'Ha', the team starts to become independent and does not need the daily handholding or instructions as they have acquired some mastery. For example, the team may not require the Agile coach's guidance to conduct daily stand-ups or sprint planning but may still need guidance and coaching for complicated situations like increasing performance, friction between team members or addressing anti-Agile patterns. As an example, if the Scrum master is falling into a command-and-control way of operating, the Agile coach will then individually coach the scrum master. At the 'Ri' level, the team is completely independent, and they are even implementing their own practices. The Agile coach at this level is an advisory role where very specific issues are addressed, for example, what to do when the teams are in remote locations.

The Agile coach coaches the team, the scrum master, the product owners as well as the customer and stakeholders. They also coach the leaders of the organization; hence an Agile coach has great facilitation, mentoring and coaching skills and is often equipped with lots of experience and expertise in Agile and human psychology.

Agile coaches also may be specialized in different types of coaching. They may focus only on team level coaching or individual role-based coaching, like coaching scrum masters, product owners, etc. Also, they can focus on specific frameworks such as Scrum or Nexus or Spotify. There are also enterprise Agile coaches who specialize in coaching leaders at the executive or leadership levels to transform their organization into Agile. Enterprise Agile coaches have a vast amount of knowledge in various Agile frameworks, not just one, and business and functional knowledge as well.

Chief Agile Officer (CAO)

In some organizations where Agile needs to be applied from leadership level to the team and individual level, Agile must be led as a strategic initiative. That involves enterprise-wide strategy development, framework development, capability development and implementation. Such initiative needs to be led by a visionary leader who is equipped with strategic leadership skills and hands-on extensive Agile expertise. Such initiatives also may involve creating a Center of Agile or communities of Agile practices across the organization.

The chief agile officer is the strategic leader who leads such an initiative. Reporting to the CEO/ COO, they take the initiative of transforming the enterprise into a new way of working through Agile. You will read about this role in detail in Chapters 6 and 7.

3

THE ROAD TO ENTERPRISE AGILITY

Iused to take the train to commute to the office. One day when the train broke down halfway to my home, in an area with no access to taxis, I decided to walk home while others took the decision to wait for a replacement bus. Each passenger on that train quickly reacted to the change either by waiting for the replacement bus, calling someone at home and asking them to pick them up, or walking home. Some may have even changed their plans completely and popped into a bar to chill out.

As an individual, we can be flexible and respond to any change life throws at us. If we know the purpose and the goal, we find a way to achieve the same thing when our routine is disrupted by sudden changes. Hence, agility at an individual level is easy.

But this level of individual agility changes a little bit when we must work as a team. In a group, everyone acts differently and thinks differently; hence capability should increase, but personality differences and communication gaps can interfere and sometimes this capability may be lost in a group. However, when we find a common theme, that individual agility can be brought back again. That is what Agile can do to a team. It creates a framework where the team unites as one person through Agile values, practices, and principles so that they can achieve productivity and agility simultaneously. However, when the number of teams increases, this agility becomes weaker and weaker. That is what we see in large organizations. While efficiency, productivity, and agility are there at team level, when we move to multiple teams, business units, and finally, at enterprise level, we lose it.

However, it is an essential capability to develop as changes and uncertainties are increasing and how 'agile' an enterprise becomes is not only a competitive factor but also a survival factor. DBS Bank, one of the leading banks in Singapore and Southeast Asia, is a testament to that. It is the largest in the region, serving individual and corporate customers.

When one of the executives, Paul Coban, then COO of the organization, heard from a taxi driver, a customer of DBS, what he thought DBS stood for, 'Damn Bloody Slow', it was eye-opening (Bloomberg, J. ,2016) . They may have been the largest bank in Southeast Asia with a strong financial portfolio, 24,000 employees, many subsidiaries, and ATM machines everywhere, but for the taxi driver, none of that mattered. What mattered was that he was not getting satisfactory service from this large corporation.

When organizations grow bigger at the national, regional, or international level, instead of increasing agility, they lose agility. Yet, enterprise agility is a capability that organizations need to increase, not decrease.

Enterprise Agility

How do we know if an organization is Agile or not? There are certain characteristics that demonstrate enterprise agility as explained in the table below. It is possible to have other capabilities besides those listed, depending on the type of business or the nature of the company, however, these are some common ones.

Flexibility	This is the flexibility of the organization's business model, products, systems, workforce, structure, and business strategies. As an example, how flexible they are to create a new product portfolio without impacting the rest of the business or products, how easy or difficult it is to merge or split the business into other units, etc. In some organizations, we have seen that some business activities or departments operate the way they do because of the financial model. So, their operational model is tightly coupled with the financial model, which does not allow for a swift operational model.
Responsiveness	Responsiveness refers to reacting quickly to changes in the customers' preferences and demands. It also means the ability to react quickly to changes in the market and the business environment, as well as to social and environmental issues. In addition, responsiveness describes the ability of a business to adjust its objectives or goals in line with emerging changes.

Culture of change	This refers to an environment supportive of experimentation, learning, and innovation. This means a positive attitude to changes, new ideas, people, and technology. It also encompasses continuous improvement, learning and employee training, and change management. As an example, do employees, along with leaders, take change as a positive experiment that they must explore, or do they see it as 'ah, yet another thing'?
Speed	This refers to the shorter cycle time of value delivery. When applied at the enterprise level, can the enterprise deliver strategic value within the organization in a shorter period? As an example, if the organization finds a business opportunity in another country, can the employees exploit that opportunity within a shorter period of time without impacting the rest of the customers or businesses?
Integration and low complexity	This refers to intra- and inter-enterprise integration. Can people, systems and processes respond to sudden changes or not? Does communication flow seamlessly or filter through many layers? How easy is it to integrate systems or disintegrate systems? Is the structure complex or simple enough so that external events can be easily supported?

Mobilization of core competencies	This means that an organization should have the following:
	Diversity of skills which can be mobilized to respond to changes
	Capability of mobilizing people for upscale and downscale ventures
	Capabilities to merge with other businesses
	Capabilities to integrate and disintegrate with partners, vendors, or customers

Achieving agility at enterprise level is a challenge when the enterprise is growing in terms of number of employees, business units, products, and services. That's the reason we can try to get inspiration from a team able to increase agility without losing efficiency, productivity, and the main reason why a team exists: to serve the customers.

Benefits of Enterprise Agility

Multiple empirical studies reveal the benefits of enterprise agility. The McKinsey research with 22 C-level executives across six sectors demonstrates that adopting Agile at enterprise level increases financial performance by 20 to 30%. This financial performance is a result of overall customer satisfaction, which leads to an increase of sales through repeating customers and loyalties. It also reduces the marketing, branding and discounting costs required to retain customers. Internally, employee satisfaction increases, hence the cost of rehiring is reduced, resulting in cost savings there, too. Other empirical research reveals that organizations with strong enterprise agility generate revenues 37% faster, with a profit that is 30% higher than those of non-Agile companies (Glenn, 2009; Wang et al., 2014).

These productivity and quality improvements are a result of fewer human errors due to automation as part of innovative ideas coming from collaborative knowledge workers, who are able to make decisions by themselves (rather than waiting for decisions from leadership, thereby reducing the time taken to act) and decreasing delays by breaking down silos through cross-functional work. These improvements contribute to reducing CAPEX and OPEX, which are measured by leaders, or increasing other metrics like the Net Promotor Score (NPS).

The findings of the 14th State of Agile Report as illustrated below, give a clear picture.

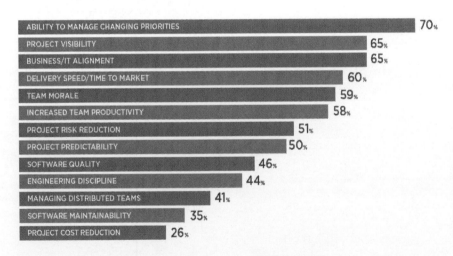

Figure 19 : Benefits of adopting Agile –
(14th annual State of Agile Report 2020 as retrieved from Digital.ai)

The benefits of applying Agile across the organization are multifold. One leader who implemented Agile at his business unit told me, "Even a small bit of Agile application gives us massive benefits". He is working for a global company with more than 300,000 employees who develop integrated solutions for the energy sector. The solutions they build are used to control industrial turbines and windmills in industrial mechanical plants. He applied Agile to his department of nearly 30 employees and the benefits were noticeable. The employees never needed to work overtime after the Agile implementation, so they were happy and indirectly the retention rates increased. In a country (India) where talent competition was high, the increased retention gave indirect benefits of reduced cost of re-hiring and retaining the knowledge capital in the organization. Customers who used their solutions were content as the department was able to accommodate their changes and give solutions to the tethering problems they identified in the industrial plants which increased customer satisfaction, Net promoter score.

Agile benefits are visible and the cost of not thinking about enterprise agility may be high. Companies are facing unimaginable threats to their survival through technology disruption, climate change, business model changes and workforce changes with millennials, who will be 75% of the workforce by 2025, moving away from corporate careers. (Haworth & Work Collectiv, 2017)

Enterprise Survival During Unprecedented Times

History tells us that no company is too big to collapse. The Fortune 500 company statistics give us some evidence. The data shows that the life span of Fortune 500 companies has shrunk in recent years and is continuing to shorten, as depicted in the graph below.

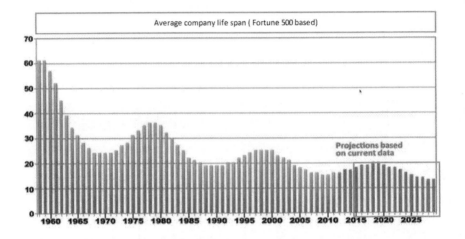

Figure 20 : Average life span of fortune 100 companies

Although some of these companies used to have longer lifespans prior to the 1980s, since then, they have become shorter and shorter. Blockbuster, the home movie and video game rental services giant, Kodak, once the world's biggest camera film companies, and Lehman Brothers Holdings Inc., etc., are a few examples of companies that disappeared from the list.

Staying in the limelight is not guaranteed. In 1996, General Motors, Ford, Exxon, Walmart, and AT&T took the top five positions in the Fortune 500.

RANK ∧	NAME	REVENUES
1	General Motors Corporation	168,828.6
2	Ford Motor Company	137,137
3	Exxon Corporation	110,009
4	Wal-Mart Stores, Inc.	93,627
5	AT&T Corp.	79,609

Figure 21: Fortune 5 in 1996

But ten years later, AT&T lost its position to Chevron. Twenty years later, Ford, General Motors, Chevron, lost the top five positions, making space for Apple, Berkshire Hathaway, and McKesson.

1	Walmart
2	Exxon Mobil
3	Apple
4	Berkshire Hathaway
5	McKesson

Figure 22 : Fortune 5 in 2016

Twenty-five years later, in 2021, regrettably, Exxon Mobil, Berkshire Hathaway and McKesson lost their positions to Amazon, CVS Health and United Health groups. The tech companies Apple and Amazon were not in the list ten years prior. What market position a company holds is just a monetary thing and they are not guaranteed a permanent position in the prestige club. Some companies realize this in a very painful way. IBM is an example.

In 1970, IBM was in the fifth position on the Fortune 100 list, the only IT company in the top ten list. But in 1980, it dropped to eighth position on the list. In 1990, it went up again and took fourth position, then in 2000, moved back to sixth position. In 2010, it lost its position in the top ten and moved to 15th position. When companies like Apple, Google, Facebook, and Amazon were starting to take the lead in the Fortune 100 list, IBM, which had once been the only IT company on the list, was losing its position.

IBM is not a small company. Its history dates to 1891 and, for a period of time, it managed to be part of historical moments in the USA and a few other countries as well. Its first personal computers, IBM mainframe machines, were essentials in the business world, and it was even involved in the mission to send a man to the moon in 1969. By 2010, IBM had more than 400,000 employees worldwide, but nonetheless, it was in decline. In fact, this decline started in 1990. The history books say this was due to IBM's failure to recognize customer's lack of interest in mainframe computers. It was also partially due to the poor partnership deals it had with partners such as Intel.

Another factor that contributed to the decline was employee dissatisfaction. In the early days, employees who joined IBM were set for their entire lifetime. They were paid well and young individuals who joined IBM for their first job retired in the company after thirty or forty years. That was how well IBM managed to build trust amongst employees.

But that changed. Employees who once trusted the company started to lose faith in it in the 1980s.

The company's decline, which began in 1990, was reflected in 2010 with significant revenue loss. (IBM did, however, come back and gain the 11th position in the Fortune 100 list in 2020 after making some changes, including a new way of working and strategic changes, which you will read about later).

Hence, irrespective of its size, a company can fail. In fact, getting larger is something to be concerned about as strategic leaders at the top can lose sight of their main purpose as they are too removed from the customers. They cannot take the pulse of the customers, resulting in slow strategic changes to respond to customer needs. Also, they are far away from the employees who makes things possible. As a result, strategies may not reflect the customer needs or the employee's insights.

I remember a heated debate that took place a few years ago in one of the companies I worked for.

This company was a Fortune 100 company that had been in that position for over a hundred years. It had more than 80,000 employees at the time and major strategic decisions were made at the headquarters in the USA. They decided to roll out a massive business transformation program. The solution was designed and developed in headquarters, and then they started rolling out to each country. But employees complained about the solution. To face their resistance, one of the executive leaders from headquarters flew to a middle eastern country and asked all the employees in the region to gather so that she could explain why they were doing the transformation program. One of the employees from the region asked, "Can you tell us how you reached the conclusion that this solution is going to work for us? Even though in this country we contribute 5% of the revenue of the company by serving 17% of the entire customer portfolio, no one asked us if this would work for us and our customers. And after three months using this as a test system, I can tell you it is not working for us or our customers." Applause exploded throughout the room and the executive leader had to pause to collect her thoughts before crafting an answer.

Hence, leaders at the strategic level need some connection to the workers and customers at the ground level. They need to ensure smooth, quick communication and information flow between these two layers, so that strategies are not made in isolation and far from the reality of the situation. In this example I just gave, the executive leader replied, "When we make strategic decisions, we don't need to talk to everyone." Someone booed. The transformation that they initially planned to complete in two years was stopped after five years because it was not working for the employees. But the damage was unrecoverable. Many employees left, close to 30 billion US dollars had been sunk, and the company's lack of growth was reflected in the financial market as depicted in the graph below.

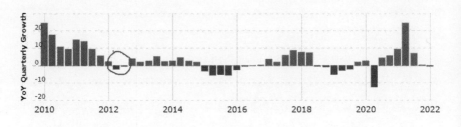

Figure 23: The financial impact during the transformation program

This case is just one among many and is typical when the scale of the company increases. Hence, breaking this vicious cycle is something leaders must think through.

One company which has been able to identify the 'risks of scale' and tried to mitigate them without becoming less agile is Google. Google's split and the birth of Alphabet is a good example of strategic agility and nimbleness at the strategic level.

Google as an Example of Strategic Agility

Can we imagine a day without using Google products? If we are on the road, we need Google Maps. If we are in a shop, we use Google Pay. If we are just passing time, we browse Google. If we are bored, we go to YouTube. The list goes on. Google, which hasn't even been around for 50 years, has managed to change how the world operates. In fact, we as customers are never bored with Google products.

The founders of Google, Sergey Brin and Larry Page said, "Google is not a conventional company. We do not intend to become one." Just 22 years old, it managed to reach the 22nd position in the Fortune 100 companies list by 2020. In 2015, Google did something which some scholars define as 'strategic agility'.

Doz and Kosonen (2007) defined 'strategic agility' as the ability to exploit something to one's advantage. Strategic agility also means changing patterns and deploying resources in a thoughtful and purposeful but fast and nimble way rather than remaining hostage to stable, pre-set plans and existing business models. The way a company has been operating may not work all the time. It is necessary to avoid the comfort zone and be open to options and opportunities to avoid threats.

In 2015, Google split up and created another company called Alphabet. Co-founder, Page, wrote to investors explaining their reasons for the move:

> "We've long believed that over time companies tend to get comfortable doing the same thing, just making incremental changes. But in the technology industry, where revolutionary ideas drive the next big growth areas, you need to be a bit uncomfortable to stay relevant." (Larry Page, 2015, G is for Google. Retrieved from https://abc.xyz/)

Their CEO, Sunder Pichai, was doing an incredible job taking the lead at Google but the co-founders still decided to split the company.

As Page explained, Google was growing bigger and bigger. Focusing on the next level of innovation under the same gigantic structure was complicated. Hence, the co-founders decided to fully focus their next decade of innovation on the life sciences sector and healthcare-related matters. They asked Sunder to lead Google while Sergey and Larry focused on Alphabet. (Larry Page, 2015, G is for Google. Retrieved from https://abc.xyz/)

And what was the result? In 2015, Alphabet (Google then) was in the 40th position on the Fortune 100 list but just six years after this strategic move to be 'big-small', Alphabet moved to ninth position (2021). IBM, which went downhill in 1990, did a similar thing after realizing the truth.

IBM and Lenovo

International Business Machines Corporation (IBM) was known for its mainframe machines. The sale of personal computers was also a major part of its business operations until 1981. It was the largest PC manufacturer next to Microsoft and Intel. As of 2004, IBM's PC business generated 12% of its 92-billion-dollar annual revenue. But, in 2004, IBM sold its PC business to Lenovo. Considering the revenue this unit generated, which was a little over one-tenth of its total revenue, this shift was massive. Yet this strategic movement was required.

With the shift, IBM decided to invest in the future. It focused on research and development and made Watson, which is a Machine Learning and AI platform. Then it invested heavily in developing cloud platforms and creating new capabilities through IBM Interactive Experience (IX) and IBM Garage, which became its human-centric design division and its start-up way of providing solutions, respectively.

Releasing its grip from a marginal profit-earning business allowed IBM to free its resources and divert the energy to build what is required for the future. And that is part of strategic agility: how quickly strategy can be rerouted to respond to anticipated future trends, threats, opportunities, or risks. When rerouting strategies, organizations may even need to change their organizational structure. ING Direct is a good example.

ING Direct

Founded in 1991 in the Netherlands, ING bank now operates in six regions and has more than 54,000 employees. In 2020, its revenue was estimated at €18 billion, and it is one of the top 30 largest banks in the world. Reaching such height in just thirty years is something significant. There is some connection to the way they operate using Agile and Agile practices.

Although ING was financially well off, there was one thing that kept its leaders sleepless at night. They noticed that customer behaviors change rapidly. As a company completely dependent on customers, their biggest threats, as well as opportunities, came from their customers. ING realized that customers didn't have any reason to stick with them in a world where more customized financial services were emerging from fintech start-ups.

This perspective made ING think differently. They tried to find out how to provide more value to their customers rather than just processing their transactions, deposits, and withdrawals. Was that the only thing they could do for them? ING realized that instead of just conducting business transactions such as savings and paying interest, they could make it possible for their customers to increase their wealth as well. So, the company decided to focus on this.

But it is not that easy to be 'customer focused' because customers change their minds so rapidly, all the time. So much waste is generated when they change their minds and due to the speed at which their behavior changes. ING tried understanding what was preventing them from responding quickly to the customers' changing behaviors. They did an end-to-end value stream mapping, and the results were insightful.

The way their organization was structured resulted in departmental silos. Work was done department by department and the handling per department took a long time. Each department had their own processes, procedures, and SLAs, and they followed those SLAs, not what was required to respond to the customer. Collaboration between departments was minimal, and if any existed, it was formal. Also, the decision making was kept at the leadership level, hence the employees on the ground facing the customers had to wait till the decision passed to them through the siloed departments.

They realized this structure was hindering their flexibility and ability to respond to customers' changing requirements. So, they decided to change the hierarchical structure and give away decision-making powers at leadership level. Instead, the employees closer to the customers became the decision-makers. It was a radical and bold move.

They adopted a flat hierarchy to gain operational agility and make the processes lean, customer-centric and value-based, influenced by the Spotify model. The smallest unit, the squads, which consisted of seven to 11 cross-functional (business + IT) team members, were given the accountability and ownership of a service/product or a problem to solve.

Managers did not interfere; the squads took ownership. They fuelled the 'power of small'.

When attempting to scale this approach, ING found that one squad was not sufficient to solve bigger problems like an enterprise-level initiative. So, without losing the power of the small, cross-functional team, they grouped multiple squads working on a product into a tribe. To ensure each squad member was given the necessary support in terms of career guidance, coaching, mentoring and skills development in the area of their choice, they also created chapters. A chapter leader was the mentor or coach for each chapter rather than a general manager. This simple structure gave the organization flexibility and empowerment. It was enough for them to be productive and effective.

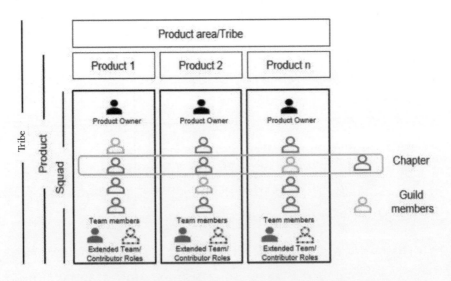

Figure 24: The organizational structure using Spotify

Then they hacked the culture. They removed the walls and partitions which separated people and created more collaborative open workplaces where employees could mingle. This allowed the creation of social spaces and free information flow at every level.

This kind of change required an existing culture to be rewired in the right direction. And that started from top to bottom. To date, ING leads the way as a different kind of bank — a bank that has the customers as its 'north star'. As a result of this progressive approach, ING has become an industry leader that is not scared of uncertainties or disruptions because they have the necessary agility across the framework of their whole organization to react, adjust and thrive when faced with adversity. What DBS bank did was something similar.

DBS Bank Singapore

Just like ING Direct, DBS also adopted the mindset of scaling up the power of small. They came up with the slogan: 'DBS is a start-up run by 22,000 people'. In order to make each of their employees a leader, they began to empower them. DBS took their lead from the culture of start-ups: bursting with energy, experimental and innovative while being small. Start-ups fail and learn, then succeed and deliver faster and better results. If there is anything to learn from start-ups, it is the power of small which drives passion, agility, flexibility, innovation and lack of bureaucracy, all qualities most large organizations struggle with.

Also, instead of assuming what the customers needed, DBS Bank started asking their customers if they were getting what they wanted and how they could serve them better. They built the unique capability of user experience research and hired a bunch of user experience researchers as they wanted insights from the customers and to design the products and services according to those insights. That was a culture change. Rather than the bank designing the products and making it available to the customers, they did things the other way. They asked what products would serve the customers better and rewired everything to design the product and services needed by the customers. Then they implemented lean Agile which accelerated that product design, development, and delivery; it happened from top to bottom.

Ten years later, DBS Bank has undergone more massive changes, both internally and externally. If you step into a DBS Bank today, you won't feel like you're in a bank. Instead, you'll feel like you're in a tech company in Silicon Valley. How customers do banking has changed. It is now not a must to visit the bank to get a loan anymore. In fact, in some countries, DBS have removed physical branches entirely. They have changed how they recruit people — the process has gone from a few months to only a few days. It has become a place where people love to work. As a result of these and consequent changes, there was a general improvement in the bank's performance, and in 2017, Euro Money named DBS as the World's Best Digital Bank (Jelassi, T et al,2020).

In the journey toward becoming an Agile organization from top to bottom and bottom to top, an agility mindset must be cultivated and encouraged at all levels. This is what we call strategic, business, and operational or delivery agility.

4

BUSINESS AGILITY

Neil was a software engineer with a decade of experience. He had a reputation for his expertise and also for his criticisms of every possible thing on the planet. He was very confident of the work he was doing and believed his company needed his skills; hence his company was working for *him*. He couldn't be blamed. He was a millennial. As his company was a professional services company, his thinking was right.

The company sent him as a consultant to a client location and Neil solved the clients' problems. In return, a consulting company charged a consultation fee from the client and it was three times Neil's salary. In other words, Neil was an asset and a money machine. His daily rates were high as he was one of the best engineers. So, he was right, the company needed him.

He worked at the client site for more than two years and he had no reason to come to the headquarters of the professional services company. But one fine day, Neil sent an email to the HR department. In the email, he informed them of a discrepancy in his pay slip. His salary should have been 8K per month, but he noticed he had been paid only 7K for the last 12 months. He saw this when he was filing his tax returns. In the email he explained the issue and asked for the reason he was getting 12K less than what he was supposed to get.

Neil got a reply from the HR department instantly. Quite a surprise. Except it was an auto reply from the system. The email thanked him for contacting them and explained how they received many queries so they would need three days to get back to Neil.

Neil understood. He waited for three days. Nothing happened. So, he sent another follow-up email. He got the same automated response. After another two days, now more than six business days, Neil composed another email and addressed it to the director of HR, the director of the payroll department, and copied in the CEO. In the email, Neil explained that the company had breached the labor law by not paying him what was agreed in the contract. And still, after six working days, apart from an automated email, he had not had any update as to whether someone was looking into it or not. He explained how it was not acceptable. This was a company that promised clients they could help reform and optimize HR functions, but the same company had not even dealt with an HR issue in six days; a critical issue faced by an employee who was bringing a monthly revenue of 18K to the company. He hinted he would be taking legal action.

The HR director was pissed off. "Neil has a terrible attitude," he concluded after talking to Neil's manager. "Why did he have to copy in the CEO? Doesn't he understand we have more than 200,000 employees? Can't he wait?" It's hard to believe that was the HR director's response!

I have many similar stories, but one of my personal experiences with a global company is somewhat ridiculous and humiliating. I applied for a leadership position a few years ago, and I was contacted by the hiring manager directly. Our discussion went into three rounds of interviews, conducted fairly fast with the business unit leaders even though they were in different countries. Finally, the hiring manager called me and informed me that I had been selected and we discussed the salary details, the joining and onboarding dates. The final step was for HR to send me the offer letter. He told me someone from HR would reach out to me as he had already contacted them to collect my information. Meanwhile, I had two other offers in my hand; all I had to do was sign them, but I liked this company, and the hiring manager sounded like a person I would enjoy working with. Hence, I decided to go with this one.

Three days passed, and no one contacted me. When HR finally contacted me after five days, the HR executive told me, "We would like to set up the first round of interviews with HR and see how you fit into the culture of our organization." Well, as you can imagine, my hair stood up and, in my mind, I was trying to find the words to be polite and at the same time tell them to find someone else. I immediately decided that this company had no uniform way of working and either HR was not synced with the business units, or the business units were not synced with the HR department. If it was like that for a hiring situation, I couldn't imagine what I would be getting into working in such a company.

I should say that I crafted my language fairly decently, but I told them they should be synced with the hiring manager. I turned down the HR person's request to set up another meeting for the 'culture fit' interview round. Once I hung up, I rang the hiring manager and informed him of the conversation, which he understandably felt embarrassed about. He apologized and convinced me to take the job. I was not wrong about the company. They worked in silos; often the left hand didn't know what the right hand was doing.

What Does It Take to Be Agile in Business?

In the journey toward achieving enterprise agility, how each business unit works within the unit as well as in collaboration with other units matters as what will end up as the value to the customers or other departments/employees needs to pass through these units. Are the business units structured to provide better value to the customers or service providers? Are the service providers getting value from them? Business leaders should ask these questions if their intention is to serve customers better or at least to survive in a future world where disruptions are the only certain thing.

When an opportunity is identified, a company should be able to quickly respond by grabbing the opportunity and using it to gain competitive advantages. Doing that needs collaboration with other business units as well as within the business unit. However, the structure of most businesses, along with the way they operate, is not conducive to swiftness and nimbleness, causing days, months, and years of delays, which negatively impact the business.

It is for this reason that business divisions and functions must consider adopting Agile practices in their work, yet Agile adoption at the business division level is surprisingly slow. The Agile way of working, values, principles, and practices are applicable almost everywhere. Just applying a few Agile practices can deliver phenomenal results. Let me explain through a personal story of a business issue I managed to solve by applying a few Agile practices and hacking the culture of the HR. To protect its identity, I'll call this company iTech Consulting.

Bringing Agility to the recruitment and selection process of iTech Consulting

As the head of the digital business division of iTech consulting, one of my challenges was hiring technology experts. Human capital was our main asset. The clients we served were other global or national companies in the telecoms, banking, retail, and energy sectors. We were not a recruitment company but when these client companies started some big transformation programs like digital banking, or eCommerce development, they wanted us to provide them with strategic, as well as technology services, which included technology consultants.

When the internal consultants were already allocated to other clients and projects, iTech had no other option than to hire from the external market. Hence, being able to hire the best candidates fast was a deal-breaker. Not being able to hire the right candidate on time could cost us several million US dollars a year and the loss of any potential future opportunities from that enterprise customer as well.

I had to work with the internal recruitment division of HR, which was led by a recruitment director who reported to the HR director. Working with them was not an easy thing. Three recruiters were shared amongst other business units. Hence, they were always busy and under-resourced. At any given time, they were hiring more than 150 positions. They worked with external recruitment companies, but still they were not able to send quality resumes, and often they were not aligned to the job descriptions or the experience we were seeking. As a result, time to hire increased, and we often ended up not filling the vacancies, leading to a loss of revenue. Regardless, the internal recruitment team was always busy doing this or that, but we never seemed to get anywhere with them.

In fact, how the recruitment function worked in iTech consulting was not so drastically different from the majority of other companies. The external party involvement meant that the time to hire candidates was a longer process; on average, the time to hire in the best case was one and a half months, and in the worst case, it could even be six months. The reason why is explained in the value stream below.

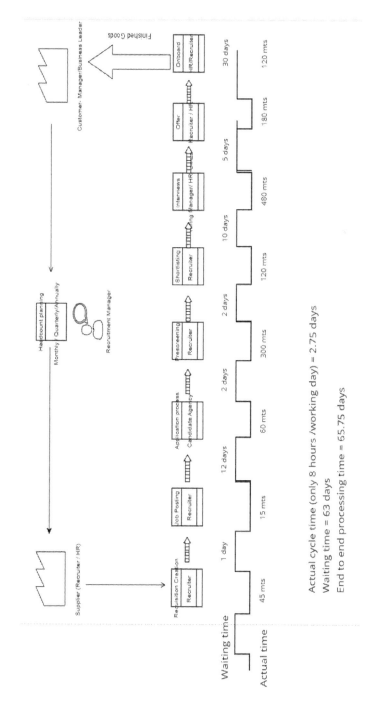

Figure 25: The value stream mapping of a typical recruitment cycle

These delays were caused due to many dependencies like:

- Dependency on external parties, which requires excessive amounts of communication and knowledge sharing orchestration
- Tight coupling with the external parties makes the process less flexible and less agile
- Lack of ownership and accountability as external parties do not own the problem; hence, the solution is not so important. It is just another transaction to them.

I was extremely annoyed about the lack of value the HR team was providing. I'd had more than 40 open positions to be filled for more than four months, and our fulfillment rate was close to zero. At one point in time, I had ten mobile developer positions to be filled, and they were vacant for more than six months. We were close to losing the commercial banking customer not only for that opportunity but also for potential future opportunities since our reputation was not so great as we were not able to provide the consultants they wanted.

At that tipping point, I introduced a few Agile practices and broke the existing unproductive process.

a. We deprioritized all the other positions and prioritized mobile developers, which was the highest critical value delivery to the customer we were working with at the time (perhaps you are wondering about the other positions and other customers. Well, the simple truth is that when you deal with limited resources, dealing with multiple equal priorities is almost equal to not delivering any value to any customer).

b. Then, we created a cross-functional team, which consisted of two internal recruiters (one for sourcing and the other for offers and onboarding) and the customer representative who had the detailed requirements for the position.

c. We made the interview process lean and reduced the waste and introduced automation:

- We used an automated coding test to validate the candidate's technical expertise.
- Those who had a pass mark were immediately invited for a technical interview with a tech lead followed by a culture fit interview on the same day.
- The gap between the technical interview and culture fit interview was just five minutes. During these five minutes, the technical interviewer passed on a quick summary and their decision on whether we should hire the candidate or not to the head of the business unit.
- Then, I interviewed the candidate for the cultural fit assessment. I had another senior manager with me, and we made the decision on the spot. We passed the decision to the offer manager to make the offer.

d. We scrapped weekly hour-long meetings. Instead, we adopted 15-minute stand-ups with two recruiters, three technical and one business interviewer, me, and an operational administrator.

The team got into the rhythm quickly, updating each other on who was available for interviewing so that we knew if someone was not available to conduct the interviews quickly and could organize another interviewer without rescheduling. Operations started moving fast. At the end of the four weeks, which we divided into one-week sprints, we had managed to make eight offers to eight candidates who joined the company after four weeks serving their notice periods.

Finally, the ten positions that could not be filled for six months were filled in two months thanks to a few Agile practices. The lesson to learn in this case is that a huge Agile adoption plan is not necessary to reap the benefits. Even just a few Agile practices, if rightly used, can deliver significant outcomes. Imagine what would be possible if these practices were applied across all the HR functions.

Why business agility should be a top priority for units like HR

The role of HR in any organization shouldn't be underestimated. For most of the internal and external candidates, HR represents the entire organization. In the recruitment process, recruiters, who are part of the HR department, are the first people the candidates talk to. In the internal world of the company, HR is one of the first places for employees to talk as well. If they are slow, if they do not deliver value, it is a reflection on the organization. That is the reason why in the previous case Neil had the right to be upset with the HR department.

However, in many companies, the HR department is under-resourced (hence they outsource). While HR provides a wide array of services to the internal employees and external employees, its complexity, human capital issues and lack of resources are not an excuse as many internal functions depend on them. That is exactly the reason why HR should find ways to bring agility to deliver value to customers/employees and help the organization's scaling agendas. Otherwise, how could an organization like Amazon grow to the level where they are now?

The other complexity is that the future workforce will be completely different to the current workforce,

Five years ago, you might not have heard about 'social media strategists', 'AI engineers', 'block chain developers', 'content moderators', 'cloud engineers', 'vloggers', 'evangelists', etc. But currently these are the latest jobs in the market and companies need them, hence HR needs to help the business to hire these talents. However, two-thirds of the future workforce will not want to work for big corporations and that will be a different generation HR has to cater to. So, how can HR be ready to attract profiles like this to support the growth targets of their enterprise?

One of the important things HR needs to do is change their culture. For many people, HR is more of a secret, controversial, political place than a transparent place. HR departments are not renowned for speed. The diagram below shows the result of empirical research I conducted with 123 people.

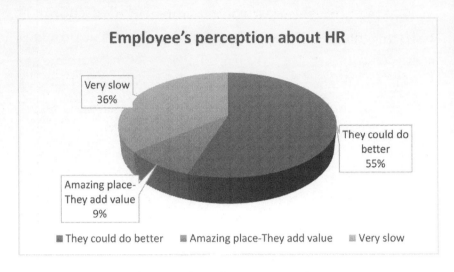

Figure 26: Employee's perception about HR

So, how can the HR department change this perception and add value for the internal and external stakeholders? The HR department should find ways to collaborate with others internally and externally and explore opportunities to automate the non-value-adding repetitive tasks (such as pre-screening candidates and reference checks or completely debunking reference checks and background checks when they are not required). They should make the department a transparent and trustworthy, welcoming place that develops practical policies. These should include finding ways to challenge the existing processes by taking innovative approaches which work for individual employees. Each employee has different requirements and situations, and one policy may not be applicable to all, leaving some employees feeling neglected and like they are not valuable to the company. This will lead to increased turnover. In a world where the gig economy is moving forward aggressively, employees no longer need to work in big companies if it doesn't work for them. HR needs to get insights from its employees and act swiftly.

While Agile principles, values, and practices greatly aid with these cultural changes, frameworks like Kanban can help immensely to add operational agility to the daily work. As I demonstrated in the previous case, even a few, small Agile practices can deliver great benefits. Now let's explore where Agile has been applied in other areas and how it has helped achieve business agility.

Credit risk management and Agile

Let's assume you apply for a housing loan from a bank. Usually, the bank will take from four days to eight weeks to approve the loan request. In some countries, this time can be even longer, and this period is a nail-biting period for you (the customer). Why does it take such a long period to approve a loan? This is because the bank must do a background check such as a credit analysis of the customer, land valuation, repayment assessments, etc. Even so, should it really take such a long time? The answer lies in the process the bank follows when the customer submits a loan application.

After you submit the application to your financial advisor, all loan applications collected during that day are sent to various departments for further processing. One such department is the credit risk management team. The credit risk management team, which is a back-office function, receives hundreds of loan applications in a day, possibly from other branches as well. So, your application will be in the queue until the assessments of the other applications are completed.

When your application is picked, the risk assessor needs the right level of information to assess the credit history, property valuation, etc. Let's say some information is not clear or further information is needed. The risk assessor will call the financial advisor and request the necessary information or documents, and then the financial advisor whom you are dealing with needs to call you to get this information. Until that happens, your application will be put aside.

If you manage to provide the right information, then the risk assessors will resume processing the application. But, by this time, two to three weeks could have gone by. Worse still, if more information is needed, the processing will be delayed further. If this is for a hot property where other buyers are lined up with cash, you will probably lose the property by the time your loan is approved by the bank. Why does it have to be a linear process? Can your housing loan application be processed on the same day? It is clear this linear process needs to be disrupted, and a way found to minimize the delay and optimize this service.

Agile, along with innovative and collaborative approaches, could make a difference, especially in an area like loan applications where multi parties, such as the following, are involved:

- Employers for salary and employment details
  Financial institutes for credit histories

- Land registries and local councils for title and property details
- Legal representatives for contracts and relevant legal documentation
- Customer
- IT services for the necessary IT services, probably for automating the processes.

In this case, collaboration and integrations with multiple parties outside the bank from which you have requested the loan are required. Transparent, value-stream driven, inter-party (bank, land registries, government agencies, etc.) teams could identify these functional and enterprise silos and then break the silos and delays, finding ways to build innovative solutions together.

Just imagine you walk to the bank and submit your application for a loan, and within four hours, your loan is approved or rejected. Or in another case, you apply for a loan on the web or on your mobile and within a few hours or less than a day, your loan is approved. When we do ideations with customers, we discover that these scenarios are in line with customers' expectations.

Leaders and organizations that understand this are now making concerted efforts to get other business divisions on board. So far, the results are astonishing. An example of this is a financial institute that introduced the Agile way of working to its corporate audit department.

Business agility in corporate auditing

Back in 2000, I was working for a bank. Toward the end of August, we were informed that the audit process would start soon and that PwC auditors would be arriving. At the beginning of September, a team of seven auditors arrived at the bank. They worked behind a closed door in a meeting room allocated only for them. Occasionally they came to us asking for different reports or asking questions on some data, and they continued doing that for six months. After six months, they submitted the final audit report to the senior executives. Twenty years later, this process has not changed in that bank or in the global company where I am working right now. That is because the normal internal audit process is the linear, Waterfall process outlined in the illustration below for one department.

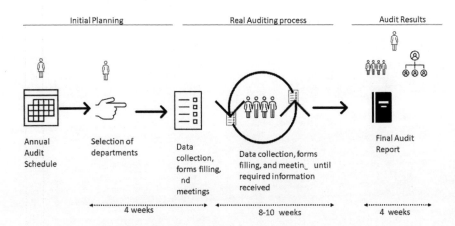

Figure 27: Traditional internal audit process

The auditor can audit only three departments maximum due to the time it takes. However, this financial institute asked the bold question, why can't Agile be used to reduce this time frame if it can deliver solutions in 30 days in the IT department? They decided to do an experiment and hired an Agile coach to figure out how to apply Agile to the internal audit process.

They adopted Scrum as their framework. This was then followed by training and coaching of the auditors and other members of the department they selected to audit. Then they selected a cross-functional team with the three auditors, three people from the department, and a scrum master to lead the Scrum process. They adopted weekly iterations and Agile practices like working in a small cross-functional team, planning for the week, daily stand-ups, and weekly showcases and retrospectives. Their process looked like the figure below.

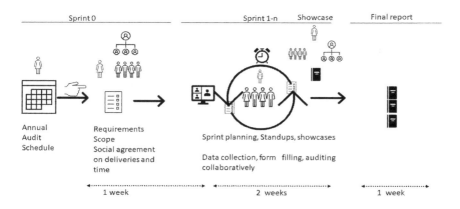

Figure 28: Agile audit process with the Scrum framework

They managed to deliver the final audit report four weeks from the start of the pilot. For this pilot, where Agile had not been used for such work before, the results were promising as it cut down the end-to-end audit cycle from 16 weeks to four weeks. That means the auditor could conduct 12 internal audits in the space of time that was used for three internal audits prior to that experiment.

As a result, the number of audits the company could do increased and employees in the impacted departments were happier as it did not involve long processes and the production of many reports. Instead, only the necessary reports were created and through this transparent process, things did move fast. The enterprise's financial position improved because they were compliant in all departments within a shorter period of time.

Summary

Business agility is becoming crucial in business units that need to move fast to provide value to internal as well as external customers. It is necessary to break the functional silos and inter-team delays to provide proactive and reactive responses efficiently and productively. While some Agile frameworks like Spotify-based chapters, squads and guilds aid in breaking departmental silos, frameworks like LeSS and SAFe can enable companies to align and unite many departments in the value stream in a mission to deliver value. Frameworks like Scrum and Kanban, on the other hand, are applicable at any level to reduce waste and deliver value faster. Agile practices can be helpful at every level of the organization and at individual levels to harvest a new culture of autonomy, empowerment, transparency, and individual leadership at an atomic level, which is essential for scaling up.

5

EXTRAORDINARY AGILE APPLICATIONS

A gile applications are emerging in industries where we would never expect to find them. Some have been pilots while others have gone beyond the pilots to the level where Agile is the way of doing the daily operational work at strategic and operational levels. Some of these applications are published in academic journals while some are published and presented at Agile or industrial conferences. Some stories are extraordinary but convincing; Agile can do a lot more to deliver better outcomes, transforming businesses so that they are agile and nimble.

Some of these stories are emerging from pioneering car manufacturers, oil and gas energy source providers, and military aircraft manufacturers. One common theme emerging from all these stories is that the trigger to move to the Agile way of working is connected to technology disruption, climate change, or natural resource limitations. In the last few decades, the automotive industry has been taking giant steps in terms of transforming the industry to face Industry 4.0. Starting from driverless vehicles to zero carbon emissions initiatives, companies are working to improve the driving experience and gain socio-economic benefits. In these innovative processes, Agile has been instrumental for industry leaders like Chrysler, Jaguar Land Rover, BMW, Volkswagen, and Porsche.

Similarly, energy source providers in oil & gas, mining & metal are challenged by global climate change as well as natural resource shortages. They may have been global giants in the past, but that may not be the case in the future if their businesses continue to execute the same business model. Their challenges are no longer at the company level (achieving competitive advantages or returning shareholder investments) but at the global, planetary level, impacting every human being in one way or another. It has become a necessity for them to change their business models and identify alternative paths, which require strategic initiatives.

In the next few pages, you will read a few stories from industries you may not have imagined Agile could be applied to.

Agile in Car Manufacturing: The Volkswagen We Campus

The We Campus in Berlin is the first initiative by Volkswagen to transit into the new way of working. As early as 2015, Volkswagen started the formation of the unit to spearhead this initiative. By 2019, this unit was made up of almost 900 professionals.

The purpose of the We Campus initiative is to leverage on Volkswagen's 'modern digital workplace' aimed at keeping up with the demanding pace of emerging innovative products, which are constantly being disrupted by newer technology. We Campus adopts Agile principles and practices. The Campus consists of multidisciplinary teams of seven to ten members working in an iterative fashion. Volkswagen calls these teams 'two-pizza teams'. The two-pizza team concept comes from Amazon founder Jeff Bezos who insisted his meetings should have only enough people to be fed by two large pizzas.

From that small unit in 2015, the We Campus has scaled up to become an Agile Center of Excellence (ACoE) with its own set of Agile practitioners. These practitioners provide their Agile expertise to other product teams who are tackling different innovative products. The ACoE offers the following services to teams/projects who are transiting into the Agile way of working:

- Provision of inter and intra team network building aimed at breaking silos and knowledge transformation throughout the We campus
- Promotion of Agile methods, practices, problem-solving facilitations
- Enabling business leaders to act in an Agile way by helping them with Agile practices, etc
- Developing processes in an Agile way and experimenting with the right processes.

With regards to specific skills required by teams in an organization, the ACoE has developed quite a few of them in areas such as design thinking, Scrum, extreme programming, Kanban, SAFe, LeSS, Nexus, Scrum@scale, etc. Organizations

127

can choose from this range depending on the type of team and the product to be worked on.

What is interesting to note about the Agile at We Campus is that Agile is applied at different levels. While the teams are fully operating in an Agile way by adopting the Agile frameworks, practices and mindset, these practices have also been scaled up to leadership level. Setting up an ACoE to develop capabilities required by other teams and leadership is a smart move from a practitioner's point of view as leadership does not have the time or expertise to develop the capabilities required in terms of Agile.

Agile in the Aerospace Industry

Delays in commercial aircraft product development are not an uncommon scenario. One reason for such delays is complex integration issues, exactly like in software development. IT systems basically must integrate many components, backend, and frontend, and they must interact with other systems. When these systems are developed by multiple parties or vendors, the complexity increases due to the synchronization needed between these parties. One team may need some components from developments from a vendor team, but the vendor team may have delays, and when the parts are delivered, they may not fit the requirements of the integration team. This will increase back and forth communication, and delays will be incurred due to these dependencies. The testimonial for this is the continuous delays of the world's largest passenger aircraft, A380. Emirates was one of the very first airline companies that placed orders with Airbus in 2007. However, the aircraft was only delivered in 2008. The delay was due to an incompatibility between different computer-aided design (CAD) systems at Airbus (Carlson & Turner, 2013).

While Agile may not be able to be fully used everywhere for aircraft manufacturing, some aspects of it, such as small teams, stand-ups, and iterative planning can be used to address some of the major issues. SAAB AB, a military aircraft manufacturer, has used Agile to solve issues.

Agile at SAAB AB

The Gripen military aircraft is the world's most economical military aircraft (Janes magazine). The Swedish company SAAB AB, the manufacturer of this aircraft, gives some credit for that success to the Scrum Agile process that they have adopted for building the Gripen.

Before adopting the Scrum framework in the manufacturing process, they used a traditional Waterfall method. The F-35 Joint Strike Fighter is a product developed using that traditional method and according to SAAB, the aircraft was delivered six years later than the planned delivery date.

SAAB has many customers, mostly defense forces from around the world. When a customer wants to add a new aircraft to their portfolio (generally the national air forces), they approach SAAB. The order could be to modify the existing aircraft purchased from SAAB or to purchase a brand-new aircraft. Like any customer-driven product manufacturing firm, SAAB's challenge is to fill customer orders on time, on budget, and meet customer specifications. They need to do this faster and better with minimal or no waste. The tougher challenge is doing that when the customer requirements are unclear and accommodating changes in the middle of the manufacturing process.

SAAB's manufacturing process used to be a linear one and consisted of integrations of many systems like:

- Main systems which control the entire aircraft from engines to the fuel control system
- Testing systems before the final integrations
- Systems that analyzed the aircraft's technical functionality and maintenance
- Systems used to integrate and coordinate planning and execution of tasks
- Pilot training systems.

Hence, when a change occurred, it created ripple effects, and other subsystems needed to be changed. Other than just developing the systems, in the process they also had to comply with heavy regulations for military aircraft.

These regulations, such as RTCA/DO178C, vary according to the aircraft type. Depending on the regulations they have to comply with, systems can be categorized into different classes: A, B, C, D, and E. A to C are treated as critical flight safety, while D and E do not affect flight safety. This means systems classed A to C need to be detailed to the atomic level, where every action/movement from requirements to implementation to operations must be traceable.

While for customers, a process might be a matter of "just changing a few lines of code", it was not the case when all components of the software or aircraft had to be traced back to every action executed (Saab Aircraft, 2020). It was complicated. The regulations, changing requirements from the customers, and the rework required to be compliant after the changes, kept the delivery delays from months to years, which forced SAAB to consider alternatives to the V model of development they previously followed.

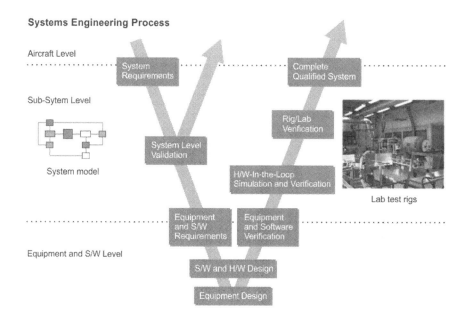

Figure 29: The traditional V model followed by SAAB.

This alternative was the Scrum framework. SAAB's experiments using Scrum in the development process started as a pilot until they were convinced it was a much more flexible, effective method compared to the V model. Most importantly, Agile addressed SAAB's pain points, which were constantly changing requirements and uncertainties coming from the customer's side.

SAAB's Agile movement included forming small cross-functional teams, scrum-based practices, such as daily stand-ups and iterative planning, scrum of scrums, inter-team collaboration, and customer integration into the teams, which increased collaboration with the customer. Integrating customers into the team helped them to reduce changes emerging later as customers were able to see the product in development from day one and clarify misunderstandings in the requirements early in the process.

Inter-team collaboration and scrum of scrums helped to discover dependencies early in the process and increased coordination between product development and software development. "Software development is not a stand-alone activity but rather a part of product development, which means that coordination with other participating processes is required. This coordination requires support between methodology and tools. Information has to be able to flow between the various processes", says SAAB.

Witnessing positive outcomes in software development and product development, SAAB then leveraged the Scrum framework for training systems as well as planning and tactical systems. Later, they scaled to the other departments which did the hardware and systems design as well.

Scrum practices of iteration-based development, creating product backlogs and planning, stand-ups and retrospectives were subsequently introduced. Even practices like pair programming were introduced.

Currently, SAAB is using the Scaled Scrum approach where more than 1,000 people are working as squads or scrum teams of seven to nine. Each team conducts their stand-ups at 7:30 am across the organization, then the scrum master of each team attends another stand-up for scrum of scrum at 8:15 am. The leaders of the scrum of scrum then attend another stand-up at 8:45 am with the leadership where leadership gets updates on any blockers at team level. The leadership can then focus on what they have to unblock, which will enable operational teams. (Rigby et al., 2018)

After its application of Agile, SAAB reported the following results:

- High level of collaboration between product owners, who were the voice of the customers, and the development team. This collaboration, which happened almost daily, helped to greatly reduce the risks of requirement misalignments.
- There was a high-level of information flow throughout the entire value stream. Hence, dependencies between teams were greatly reduced to a minimal level.
- High level of communication and knowledge transfer throughout the value stream.
- The work was divided into smaller tasks that were easier to grasp and manage.
- Team satisfaction measured from one to five, increased to 4.7.

There was also an observable difference due to the adoption of the pull system instead of the push system. In addition, high collaboration with the customer gave the teams instant gratification and the sense of being a part of a critical mission since they were directly dealing with the customers rather than through middle managers. The collaboration between other teams and the product owners helped to foster a sense of unity rather than breed division.

SAAB JAS 39E "Gripen" – Agile Design

- As per the Aviation week, the best aircraft in the world
- Cumulative program cost of $ 15 Billion
- New iteration of all systems released every 6 months
- Cost was only $ 43 Million (20% of F35)

F-35 "Joint Strike Fighter"- Traditional Design

- $143 Billion over budget
- At least 6 years late (final systems integration)
- Cost grew from $ 273 Million in 2014 to $ 337 Million by 2015

Figure 30: Traditional Vs Agile design methodologies used in aircraft design

Normally, it cost around 143 billion euros to build the F35 aircraft. But once they adopted Scrum in the manufacturing process, they managed to release an F35 every six months for only 20% of the previous cost of 143 billion. The impact was visible, transparent, and pleased the customers and investors.

Agile Transformation of Energy3000

Our next story is from a global energy company. This specific Agile application is in a department called 'reservoir management'. Let's try to understand what this department does.

Reservoir management

Oil and Gas formation began millions of years ago and can be found both onshore as well as offshore, several thousands of feet below ground level and sometimes under many thousands of feet of water. (Sergio da Cruz, 2000)

Figure 31: Vertical section of an oil and gas reservoir

Identifying oil and gas reservoirs and extraction is a complex process, and it goes through various phases known as 'exploration, discovery, appraisal, development, production and abandonment'. Exploration involves a scientific analysis of geologic structure, predictive analysis of rock formation, and extreme mathematical modeling that predicts the existence of oil and gas, how much exists, and quantities and volumes for extraction and production. According to the statistics, even such extreme analysis can go wrong. Only 30% of such predictions have proven to be accurate. Hence, one of the challenges in reservoir management is to increase the success rates of accuracy and reduce the prediction time because various factors need to be considered:

- reservoir geometry and the spatial distribution of petrophysical properties are uncertain
- fluid properties are uncertain
- measurement errors exist
- actual behavior of the rock and fluid when subjected to external stimuli is uncertain
- modelling limitations are inherent
- future prices of the product are uncertain. (Sergio da Cruz, 2000)

Achieving the right level of prediction accuracy is a tedious task and needs the close collaboration of geologists, geophysicists, geochemists, reservoir engineers, well-completion engineers, production engineers, facilities engineers, and various other professionals. These collaborators come from different disciplines, different educational backgrounds, and from different schools. The process may be linear, and not all people do the work at the same time.

Challenging times

The reservoir development department of Energy3000 was under pressure. Just some of the challenges they faced were reducing costs of operations, finding new energy sources faster and better, reducing environmental damage, compliance with various regulations, reducing health hazards, minimizing failures, dealing with rotating political parties (for approvals), increasing the accuracy of predictions, and reducing the long analysis and predictions cycles. The midstream and downstream of Energy3000 depended on the predictions given by 500 reservoir department employees located in different countries. Leaders of midstream and downstream needed 100% accurate predictions, and providing that took a long time; the minimum time for small reservoirs was at least six months, and for more complex ones, it was longer. Leaders scratched their heads when they had to think about reducing this cycle.

Could Agile help?

The leadership team of Energy3000 heard that IT teams could deliver software in 30 days using Agile as an operating methodology. "That is a phenomenal cycle time reduction," the leaders thought. They wondered if it could be applied in other areas and decided to experiment with it.

First steps

Which country would like to participate in the pilot? The global leadership team asked each country manager if they would like to be involved in the experiment. Many doubted a methodology designed for IT software development could be applicable to the work they were doing. But a few country leaders thought differently. "We are already doing many experiments. Each oil excavation is an experiment, a risk; some are successful, some are not. Why can't this also be such an experiment? What if this works?"

One country volunteered for the experiment.

It was something new that they did not have experience with, so they decided to get help from a consulting company that had enterprise-level Agile implementation experience.

The pilot

In the following week, the consultancy company collaboratively developed a plan to start the pilot, select a suitable business unit and the leadership support they needed. The plan included selecting one business case, a site for which they wanted to provide the predictive analysis and the appraisal. They also needed to organize the team, the structure of the pilot, the Agile framework, the training plan, coaching plan, and execution plan. The training and coaching plan included training all leaders from VP level to each team member level.

The leadership training introduced the Agile values, principles, concepts, and what 'being Agile' means. That included how the leader's role would change from manager to a servant leader and how they should enable the teams to be autonomous. Within the one-day leadership training, leaders practiced the Scrum way of working through a carefully developed hands-on project which taught Scrum practices.

The second step involved training the reservoir management department (phase one). They would learn the Scrum framework and practices through hands-on exercises and games. They learned behaviors like being transparent, asking for help, taking ownership of work, and being autonomous. Some behaviors were difficult to eradicate. As an example, when they found issues, they were used to not talking about them openly. The culture was that they had to try to solve issues alone. Otherwise, management might judge them. 'Fear' was something that hindered them. During the training, they understood through practice that sharing issues allowed them to gain others' help and support. Hence, as a team, they could move faster.

In the third step, a suitable business case was selected as the pilot, which could showcase the impact if Agile was successful. The business case was an actual reservoir appraisal that they had to do for one of the remote sites. They set up four weeks, two iterations for the experiment. They also set up some success criteria. If they could get the appraisal at least 50% completed by the end of four weeks, that was good enough. If the team gained the maturity to teach other teams, that was also good enough. If the leaders could decide it was possible to apply it to other divisions at the end of the pilot, that, too, was good enough. If at the end of the four weeks they did not meet the success criteria, they would stop the Agile application.

Two scrum teams were formed with two scrum masters and two product owners. Teams were given a co-creation workplace where they could work together rather than in different physical locations. That would help to reduce communication gaps as the team members sitting next to each other promoted face-to-face communication. A Kanban wall was set up in the same co-located place so that team members could update the task board promptly when a work item was finished. Also, they could see how others were progressing as well so they knew if they were proceeding as a team toward the goal or not. A cadence was set up and then the pilot kicked off with the sprint planning. The Agile coach facilitated and guided the team throughout two iterations.

Observations during the pilot

During the training

During the first part of the training given to the executive leadership, most of the leaders were surprised but convinced about the waste in the processes they followed due to context switching and communication gaps due to departmental silos. They understood departmental silos were contributing to the longer cycle times. They also realized that leadership was too much involved in the operational work where teams could manage themselves. As a result, the leadership team did not have time to do strategic work as teams were dependent on them. So, when they talked in the training about autonomous teams and empowerment of the teams, some leaders were very enthusiastic.

However, some ideas were challenging. A few leaders who had been in the company for a long time raised their eyebrows when they were told their role would become that of a servant leader. Where would the managers go if the scrum team had only the roles of scrum master, product owner, and team members? Also, how could the team be working on only one project all the time? What was meant by dedicated team? Who would do the other work coming from other teams and management if the team members were dedicated to only one project? Multitasking was necessary, some argued. But then others in the room voiced their opinions. Wasn't that the reason they couldn't finish any of the work faster? They had tried to do too many things at the same time, and as a result, nothing got finished.

In fact, there was evidence of the problem in the room itself. One of the product owners selected for the pilot (who was a manager) was missing from the two-day training because she had another set of meetings. It was essential the product owner attend the training because we taught them how to write the user requirements in the Scrum way, practices during the iteration, etc. "Oh, don't worry, I will get a debrief of the training from the team," the product owner said. "Also, can you send me the training presentation? I will catch up from that." The team which I represented from the consulting company had seen all these anti-Agile patterns before, many times, and we knew if they were to continue the way they did previously, then we were not required there, and at the same time, they would not succeed. Hence, we decided to talk to the leadership and set things straight.

We explained to the vice president sponsoring the Agile pilot how critical it was to have the product owner in the training. It was not something that could be understood from PowerPoint presentations. We gave them two options: Release the product owner from other work for four weeks (if you cannot do that, then you are not serious about this transformation), or let's select another product owner who can commit. The VP nodded and made a few calls, and we saw the product owner in the training from the next hour. In the Agile world, it is not true that leaders' jobs are disappearing. Instead, they are just doing things differently, finding ways to unblock the blockers almost instantly.

Some outcomes were unexpected. Most of the members of that team belonged to the reservoir development division. But they acknowledged that many of them didn't know each other even if they were on the same floor. Some of them had been working there for more than eight years but knew little apart from their colleague's name or the manager they were reporting to. They did not know where others were living, their interests, etc. But during the training, they got to know each other better because they were interactive during the scrum practices. Through lots of talking, they managed to break the ice and become comfortable talking to one another. There was high energy.

At the end of the two-day training, we asked them to say how confident they felt about starting their work using the practices they had just learned. Everyone in unison agreed it was a much better way to work. However, one of the senior managers who had worked in the company for two decades made a very good point.

"Anusha, I can see how this is very beneficial in IT. It is fast. I also read a book about it. It has worked in IT, and we have no doubt. But our work is not IT. This is deep-water drilling. This is like predicting which part of the moon has water, and how much water in the exact quantity. This work is complicated. So, I don't know if it can be applied."

That was a reasonable and fair comment from a leader who really loved the work he had been doing in the company for more than 20 years. We explained to him the intention of the experiment. There was only one way to know. I said, "Let's try it, shall we?" He nodded in agreement.

During the showcase

At the end of each iteration or sprint, instead of creating a bunch of presentations to showcase the progress, the team invited all the stakeholders, that is the VPs, line managers, and business unit leaders, to a demonstration of the working product. The working product in their case was the detailed plan of the reservoir, which was in Southeast Asia. The showcase was a new experience for the leadership team as well as the team.

Previously no team members had ever talked to a VP directly. In the organization's culture, VPs were at the top of the hierarchy; others were seven or eight levels below. Getting access to talk to them was not a practical thing. Executives were in a different building and did not mingle much with the people at the team or operational level. But during the showcase, that changed. All leaders, including the VPs, gathered around the Kanban wall where the team was standing up.

The room was full of artifacts they were working on. Each team member presented what they had been working on over the two weeks and the outcome of the work. Some artifacts were visualizations on where exactly the oil was present, they explained the precision level details and how they came to that level of detail. VPs asked questions and the team answered confidently. When one team member struggled for whatever reason, another member helped because he knew about it as they had been working together for two weeks. It was the effect of product planning together at the sprint planning and their status as a team that helped them to have a team-level understanding of the product they were building. So, when one team member floundered, others quickly jumped to the rescue.

The leaders were amazed by what happened at the showcase. They got to learn so much from the team that they did not know previously. They were surprised to learn that the team had reached out to other countries for their data collection so that the information they presented was accurate. The visualizations were high-fidelity data. That generated a lot of discussions and knowledge sharing between the leaders and the team because that was the information the leaders wanted. There were no PowerPoint presentations. It was just on the whiteboards or the butcher paper. Leaders took a photo from their phones so they could take the information with them. They wanted to discuss it with the rest of the leadership team.

The team had completed all the user stories they had committed to except one user story. They explained why they could not complete it. They were dependent on an external team for some input and the external team had not provided it on time, causing the delay. While in the showcase, a leader quickly rang the external team and asked them to provide the work immediately. This was an example of a leader helping to unblock an issue.

Finally, when everyone had explained the user stories and their outcomes, the leadership team praised the work. They all could see the richness of the predictions and how much work had been done within just two weeks. It was instant gratification. They could not believe that their teams had that much potential and more than anything else, how much they could achieve without the daily guidance they had given previously.

The output at the team showcase was so rich in details that the leadership team could instantly move to the next level of decision making: Where should they invest money? They also decided which sites to deprioritize as they were not profitable based on the predictions the team came up with. The leadership team was very happy. They could not stop praising the team and the team was thrilled to receive that feedback directly from the leadership team. They were the VPs, directors, and very senior people in the company and previously they did not even get to meet them. Only senior managers talked to VPs and managers transferred whatever feedback the VPs gave to the teams. Having everyone in the same room talking and listening to each other helped the leaders to understand the strengths of the team and what kind of support the team needed. Once the showcase was done, then the team sat down for a retrospective.

During the retrospective

They sat in the middle of room with lots of food and the mood was very relaxed. It was the perfect time to take a deep breath and look back at how the last two weeks had unfolded. "How are you feeling?" That was the first question I asked.

"Overwhelmed."

"It's intense."

"Focused."

"Pressured but in a different way."

"Good."

"Very different."

"Still absorbing the change."

"Happy. Really Good."

After giving these answers, everyone explained why they felt the way they did.

"It's intense because we never used to talk so much together. I felt like everyone was watching us."

"Overwhelmed because we were getting instant feedback, on the spot. Positive, though. And we're not used to that. So many new things, in fact, new ways of working, so it's overwhelming."

"We were never focused like this before. We used to receive a lot of other work, parallel work, so we never focused on one thing. But this was very focused work. That required lots of energy. But it helped to finish fast as we were focusing on getting that task done."

"I guess I said 'pressured' because of transparency. I had to provide updates at the stand-up so felt a bit of pressure. I felt pressured when I could not finish some tasks on time as I promised. But then at the stand-up, some people offered help. Later, everything got smoothed over because everyone was offering to help. It was good to be sharing the updates so we could help each other. So, the pressure reduced over time."

"Good. In fact, very good. We used to do a lot of unproductive work, emails, presentations, many meetings where we only sat and listened. Now that has been reduced."

"It's good leaders could see why we could not finish the work. There were dependencies. If external teams and partners don't get back to us on time, it is not on us. They need to help us by providing the information we need on time. So, leaders could see that, and they offered to help. We never used to have that. So, work never got finished. Now, we can finish work faster than we promised. That is, in fact, really good."

"It is really good to hear the leaders are happy with our work. We never used to talk to them like that. But now they listen. It's nice. And we (pointing at the other team members) never had fun like this before. This is intense, but it's so much fun. I guess it's because we sit in the same room with no partition between us, and we don't compete. It's a good feeling not to compete but work as a team to finish the work. It is 'us' versus 'me'. Plus, we got a lot of food. So, it was fun."

"So, do you think we should continue the same way for the next two weeks?" I asked.

They agreed in unison. *"Absolutely. This is really good."*

Then we started discussing 'what worked well' and 'what didn't work well' and 'what we can do about it'.

What didn't work according to them

Almost everyone pointed out that they were too ambitious when pulling the work. They pulled more work, assuming they would be able to finish it. But later, they understood the dependencies and the intensity of the work, so they said it was better not to over-commit but commit to what was possible and deliver it. The product owners nodded in agreement.

Then they mentioned the external meetings to which they were being invited. These external teams did not know they were in this pilot program, so when they replied late, external teams were upset with the team. So, the scrum masters decided to discuss that with the business unit leaders so they could update the external teams about the team's unavailability.

Some members pointed out that the user stories were not detailed so they almost underestimated them. They wanted more details to be added to the user story rather than just one sentence so they could be more accurate. The product owners took the action of working on the user stories prior to the sprint planning and adding more details like acceptance criteria.

After the retrospective, all the team members went out for drinks and a big feast and had a lot of fun relaxing and rewarding themselves with beer. The story continued and they kicked off the second sprint the following week with the sprint-planning session.

The outcome of the pilot

The pilot scrum project continued for four weeks. At the end of the four weeks, we collected the feedback from everyone involved in the process, from VPs down to team members. Then we collected the data points to measure the impact of any differences Agile brought to the reservoir management division as a result of this Agile way of working. These findings can be summarized as below.

Reduced cycle time

The biggest noticeable difference was around the end-to-end cycle time of the discovery and appraisal process. The discovery step included the predictions, and visualizations of the oil and gas reserves in different locations, both onshore and offshore. Appraisals included predictions on the quantity and the volume of the oil reserves and the commercial aspect, such as profitability if they were to make a commercial deal out of the reserve. All this information was included in sophisticated mathematical models and visualizations. Previously (before the Agile way), this end-to-end process of discovery and appraisals had taken at least six months. That meant only two such analyses were done per year.

As a result of applying Agile (Scrum), the same discovery and appraisal per site was done in four weeks. That meant they could do 12 discoveries and appraisals for 12 sites per year. This decreased cycle time helped the management to adjust their annual planning and the accuracy of the portfolio earlier. Not to mention if they could cover 12 sites per year, that was a competitive advantage they had over others who were trying to pitch for the same site. Anyone who could go to the government with the right level of information needed to approve the site, could get the site. If Energy3000 could do that prior to a competitor, the site would be theirs.

Accuracy and quality of work

The accuracy of the discovery and appraisals was the next item which caught everyone's attention. They noticed each prediction and each appraisal had been attacked and tackled from every possible angle. Every assumption had been identified and there was an answer for every assumption with valid data to prove it. Since the team was authorized to contact anyone in the organization to make their work successful, the team had reached out to their peer teams in places like Alaska and Houston. That had not happened previously as contacting teams outside the geographical area was the manager's job. But now there was no manager and the team who had the ownership of making the product successful did what they had to do.

The next change was related to the senior managers. They engaged frequently during the showcase, which happened at the end of every sprint. Also, now they did not have an active role in the team, when the team reached out for help, they knew they had to help. So, they jumped quickly and made themselves available (as now they had time), helping the team with whatever they wanted. That reduced the number of assumptions the team was working on. As an example, appraisals were dependent on production capacities in different sites. This information was not available to the team so when they could not get the data on time, they built the assumption "we assume the production capacity in the Java site is 50,000 barrels per day". During the showcases or at review meetings, senior managers told the team, "Ah, no, actually our production capacity in Java is 25,000 per day".

If the team had kept working on the assumption of 50K, then the rest of the work would have been a waste.

The process helped the leadership team to make quick and collaborative decisions as well. During the showcase, leaders from different disciplines joined, hence cross-functional leadership was available at the end of every two weeks. Previously this was not the case. They were very busy people. Getting a time slot in their calendar was an impossible task and getting everyone in one room was more difficult. But now this predictive cadence where the showcase was available every two weeks made them plan from their end as well. Since all leaders were present at the showcase, they could also make quick decisions after discussion during the showcase. Things moved very fast, even beyond the two teams, as leaders took the information the team presented and made it available to other teams. Positive outcomes were cascading to other areas.

Team level skill development and transformation

The next thing that was noticeable was the skills the team developed. During the Scrum process, the communication skills of the team increased tremendously. Before the pilot, some team members played a very silent role as they never had any opportunities or requirement to talk to a group. Everything was done by the managers. But during the Scrum process, each team member presented their findings to a wider audience. Some were very innovative. I noticed a girl who was very good at drawing using her skills to present her ideas. She did not use many words, but it was very visual, and others loved it and even started copying her.

The team learned how to present their ideas and findings with confidence. Fear of speaking started to disappear. The team bonding had helped them to build confidence as they knew others would help if they failed. Hence, each team member, regardless of how junior they were, developed the confidence to have a conversation or argue with the senior leaders or VPs, which they told me never happened before. They were becoming leaders.

During the pilot, the use of PowerPoint was minimal. During the entire four weeks they only used it on one occasion. It was not needed. Their work was on whiteboards or butcher paper, and they used the same during the showcases. This minimized unnecessary documentation. And when they wanted the same information, leaders just took a photo using their smartphones.

One of the leaders said to me, "I wish I could do the same. You know our life is more about PowerPoint than the actual work." Leaders, too, were learning new and better ways to reduce waste in processes.

Role of leaders

During the pilot, leaders learned to listen a lot. This was something noticeable. In that process, suddenly, the team became the central focus. As they worked as a group, they had a lot of knowledge capital, and that knowledge capital was what the leaders wanted. So, they had no choice but to listen. We saw the transition of managers and senior leaders. They suddenly did not have to hold their teams' hands. Teams learned together as they were working in small groups. But whenever they got stuck, the team did not hesitate to reach out to the leaders. Leaders helped, knowing if they did not act, everyone would know about it during the stand-ups. So, their role became more of an enabler than a hand holder. It was an eye-opening moment for the leadership team. They suddenly had a lot of time to think about strategy – the real job of a leader. They learned to trust the teams and new ways of working with the team.

To give a personal observation, I found at the beginning many leaders were insecure because in a scrum team there are no managers. They tried to enforce the same managerial style by taking a position like scrum master or product owner. Then they tried running the show as they did before. They would tell the team what to do and how to do it in a command-and-control manner. When this happened, the Agile coaches jumped in and coached the leaders to demonstrate servant leadership.

Team level burnout

The next point that was highlighted by the team was that the work was intense. That was their best way to describe it. And there were reasons for that. Prior to Agile, the results they produced took six months. Previously each member received an email asking them to do this and that and to produce this report and that report. So, they would do the analysis all alone and then schedule a call with one or another person and get the results and then write another email and send the results. If the receiver had a question, then they would write another email (or call) and the process went like that. Write an email and wait. Receive an email and try to understand what that was. Reply to the email and wait. Everything was linear. Wait and do. Now they generally had to walk to the other party the work was dependent on and have a conversation to get it solved. This was new.

However, to produce value or the working product, in this case, the final discovery analysis and appraisal in a shorter period, the wait time had to be reduced. The team had to focus on getting the work done, not sit around waiting. There was a time box: two weeks. Hence, they had to focus and make every attempt to get the work done. Practices like time-boxed talking were new. For example, they had to summarize their updates for a few minutes during the stand-up. Time was a currency which they had to use very carefully. So, it needed some careful thought to give enough details to the updates so that others could understand within a few minutes. These were new things each team member had to practice daily.

In the past, managers were the ones who talked to seniors. Team members were behind the scenes. Now, suddenly, there was no middle layer. Team members had to present to the customers, i.e., the senior leaders. So, they had to prepare; they had to practice. That was one reason the team felt it was "intense".

In addition, this new way of sitting together and collaborating with different people with different personalities was intense too. They had to tolerate the differences. They felt mental exhaustion in a shorter period. So, they felt the pressure which they explained as "intense but good". But that was at the beginning. The team soon got absorbed in the process, gained confidence, and developed the new muscle of leadership. It became their working style, and they felt happy as they achieved so much within a short period of time yet left the office at five o'clock sharp and did not have to think about work until the next day.

So, what that team experienced in four weeks was not something new. It was because they were unlearning lots of things and learning and absorbing a new way. It was like if an alcoholic used to consuming one litre of vodka in a day had to stop drinking it from the next day. The body, used to consuming alcohol for so many years, would have to unlearn and learn. But once the body got used to it, it would be replaced by a different, wonderful, beautiful feeling. That was what the team was going through.

It was unanimously agreed at every level, teams, and leadership, that Agile had made a positive difference and it could be applied everywhere. The conclusion from that pilot was "If it can be applied to reservoir management, it can be applied anywhere".

As a result, Energy3000 decided to expand the Scrum application to other departments. Within the next few weeks, an Agile portfolio was developed. Other business divisions were also mapped onto the portfolio to roll out Agile. And the reservoirs management team was appointed to train the trainers. The scrum masters who led the reservoir development team were appointed as scrum masters for other business divisions. Suddenly, they were getting new opportunities and new career development lines rather than being just geologists.

After one year of that Agile pilot, the company has now implemented Agile across other business divisions as well. They use Scrum as the basic framework and larger solutions are managed using Large-Scale Scrum.

~ SECTION 2 ~

THE ENTERPRISE AGILE JOURNEY

"I often hear leaders declare that we are now fully Agile. Well, I doubt it. Agile is not something that can be declared as an achievement or competition. It is like saying, 'I am healthy.' The truth is that we have to keep on working, day and night to be healthy. Healthiness is something to be improved on every day."

— Marcel Greutmann
— Vice President, IBM Global Business Services

6

THE ENTERPRISE AGILE JOURNEY

Where should I start? How should I start? These are some of the questions leaders have when they want to introduce Agile to their organization or their business unit. Below are some recommendations for those leaders who have these same questions.

Get a Crash Course in Agile

Getting a crash course in Agile is a good starting point to developing an awareness of the process, how and what Agile can do for your organization. Chances are high that your IT department is already practicing Agile. If that is the case, then the IT department must have Agile coaches whom you can leverage to enlighten you. If none are available in your organization, there are many available in the external community. It is not necessary to hire a consulting company to do the same. Most Agile coaches are very passionate about sharing the wealth of knowledge they have, and it is one of the reasons why Agile is so popular because coaches make tireless efforts to teach others this new and better way of working. A simple social media search for enterprise Agile coaches would give you thousands of good Agile coaches you can contact and get some help from.

Listening without any judgment is key in this process. I would emphasize the 'listening' as what an Agile coach explains may not make any sense to you at the very beginning, especially when the Agile coach is talking about dedicated teams and scrum master per team. Not having detailed plans at the beginning, leaders may take a step back, saying, "That's impossible". As an executive leader with years of experience you may feel what they are saying is not practical. But it is essential to keep an open mind as what they are explaining has been successfully used in areas we wouldn't even imagine, such as in NASA, delivering better outcomes than predecessor methods.

Make a field trip

There are many organizations that have scaled Agile to most of their departments. These companies sometimes have Agile Centers of Excellence or Agile working spaces and dozens or even hundreds of teams practicing Agile. Such companies have changed physical working spaces to facilitate the Agile way of working. As an example, figure 32 is an Agile workspace in a bank, where I led the Agile transformation.

They may have walls decorated with various posters showcasing their Agile frameworks and posters designed as part of change management activities, with post-it notes everywhere. People may be sitting in open spaces instead of cubicles. They may have different seating arrangements with beanbags or ping pong tables in the middle of the office space. And you will notice there are Kanban walls. Such workplace arrangements will give you a clue about how the collaboration happens and what facilities are required in terms of designing the workplace for maximum collaboration to break departmental silos.

Figure 32 – Agile working space

Also, you will notice people's energy. When Agile is properly in action, those who practice it are very energetic and engaged actively in their work. There will be laughter, and you will be influenced to implement a similar thing in your own organization. In my history of Agile transformations, I have yet to meet a person who wanted to go back to the old way of working (Waterfall).

Visiting one of these companies and asking them to showcase how they practice Agile may provide you with ideas, inspiration, and some sort of assurance that if it has worked for them, it could work for you too. The good thing with Agile is that it develops the community mindset. When someone wants to learn from an Agile practitioner, they always appreciate it and offer whatever help they can. Hence, if you decide to visit one of those companies and do a walk-through, they are likely to welcome you openheartedly.

Attend a Training Session

Agile is a different culture and mindset. The concepts and practices are different and somewhat new. A training session run by Agile trainers or coaches will help you understand these concepts and practices, increasing your awareness and knowledge of Agile. Although many leaders are hesitant to spend a day or two attending a classroom where they are taught the basics, once they attend, they never regret it. That is the reason some organizations, like Accenture, which I worked for some time ago, have made it mandatory that every employee, including directors and higher-level leaders, attend such training. If employees can implement those practices in their day job, they will spread them across the organization, enabling the entire company to benefit from the Agile way of working.

Start an Experimental Project

There is only one way to find out if Agile works for your organization or not. Try it out with an experiment.

This experimental project does not need to be a full-fledged one. And you can try it with a simple framework like Scrum or Kanban. An Agile coach can help you to find a good business case. It may be launching a new marketing campaign, developing a new product line, or something simple like your annual budget planning. These are very good business cases which can yield quick results. As in the case of Energy3000, discussed in the previous chapter, this kind of experiment can help to test the waters before deciding to cascade it to other areas of your organization.

Hire an Agile Coach to Help

Agile coaches are wonderful creatures, in my opinion. They are fun-loving, empathetic, happy and have a mindset always to help others. They are equipped with years of experience coaching leaders, organizations, teams and going through transformation, sometimes by leading it, sometimes helping others to lead it. Like a cricket or a baseball coach who may not be on the field playing with a cricket or baseball bat, the Agile coach may not actively be part of the Agile transformation, but they know every move and how to get the organization/teams to the next level, whatever that is. The power of an Agile coach can never be underestimated.

In one enterprise Agile implementation that involved more than five scrum teams, the product owner attended a product owner training in the middle of the program. The Agile program had been already running for nearly two months, and all the team members, including the specific product owner, were doing Agile for the first time. The Agile coach was guiding them on the Scrum framework, and almost all the team members were making progress.

However, the product owner, who came from a corporate banking background and had over a decade of experience, did not trust the team and was under pressure to showcase results to the leadership team. After attending the training conducted by a consulting company, the product owner suddenly came to the team full of energy and enthusiasm. She announced they should adopt Kanban and she wanted to scrap sprint planning and backlog planning and move into just-in-time planning with Kanban. The team was confused. First, they were wondering what Kanban was, as it was the first time they had heard about it. Second, whose lead should they follow? The product owner or the scrum master? The Agile coach was watching the drama unfolding and called for a small coaching session with the product owner, scrum master, and the team.

She gave everyone a crash course on Scrum and Kanban, explaining how it would change the program's outcome. The Agile coach asked the product owner if she still believed Kanban would solve the problem she had at hand, and the answer was "No". The team breathed a sigh of relief. If that Agile coach was not there, that Agile team could have been derailed and spent a few weeks moving to Kanban.

Agile coaches have practical experience and a depth of knowledge in various other domains like change management, human psychology, and human behaviors. Hence, most of the time they know what to do and how to help the teams and leadership to tackle difficult behavioral and process-oriented dilemmas. Getting an Agile coach to help leadership in the process of starting an Agile journey is a very good decision.

Take the leadership team on the journey

If you are very serious about Agile, one of the very first things you should consider is applying it to your way of working. It may be in your daily operational work or may be with your own executive team. Ask the question, how can you apply these practices in your daily work and with your leadership team?

As an example, Michael Holm, CEO and founder of Systematic Inc, provides some inspiration. He decided to run his executive office using Agile principles. (Darrell K. Rigby , Jeff Sutherland and Hirotaka Takeuchi, 2016) He insisted that his nine-member executive team should work exactly like a small scrum team works.

Instead of having weekly, Monday morning executive meetings, Holm started doing stand-up meetings every day. The nine-member team met for 20 minutes every day at a designated time and discussed what each of them achieved during the previous day, what they were going to do on that day and any blockers they needed to resolve immediately to enable their respective teams. This simple practice, according to Holm, was enough to be rapid and respond quickly to what needed focus. Also, since the initiative was started by the CEO, the rest of the executives willingly participated although it was something which they had never experienced before. The only way to find out if it works or not is by practicing it ourselves.

SAAB, which we discussed in the previous chapter, also did a similar thing. The executive team ran a stand-up just after teams finished their scrum of scrums, which was after the team level stand-ups. In that way, the issues and blockers at team level were escalated to the scrum of scrums and they tried to resolve them. Anything they were unable to solve escalated up to the leadership stand-up within just 90 minutes on the same day. Then the executive team could make quick decisions to unblock the blockers. The decisions were cascaded down instantly, and the teams could move on quietly as the issues were resolved. This is a very good example of the Agile way of working being spread across the organization from top to bottom.

In another financial institute in Asia, after adopting Agile, the CEO ordered that all the monthly steering committee meetings adopt Agile principles. Instead of having a bunch of presentations, he ordered all proposals come in a one pager. And then any status reports had to demonstrate how the product or service was working.

Such powerful behavioral and cultural changes are behind very successful enterprise Agile transformation. And when such changes are adopted by a leader, that is a powerful message to the entire organization, including those who resist. Such transformation must be an effort made by everyone.

Hire a Chief Agile Officer

Initial training, one-on-one Agile coaching, pilot projects and knowledge gathering will give you enough insights and confidence to see if Agile will work for your organization or not. Maybe you have already initiated the Agile rollout to a few departments like IT or operations and now you have decided it's time to implement Agile across other business divisions and across the entire organization. That is scaling up Agile across the organization.

Hence, you need someone who owns this journey. You need an executive leader to drive this across the organization. And that person is the chief agile officer or CAO. The CAO will lead the initiative, but it is essential they have backing from the CEO, COO, and the board. Starting the initiative from the executive office is a massive boost, but you cannot leave the CAO to run their own show. If the leaders of other divisions, such as the finance director or the supply chain director, have been in the company for a long time and have solid authority in their own divisions, there may be strong push backs even when CAOs start to roll out the Agile initiatives. And one way to stop such resistance is direct connection to the strategy the CEO has established. The initiatives should be driven by the CEO's office rather than just by the CAO.

However, CAOs at the strategic level with the right level of authority and the strategic view on how to scale up Agile across the entire organization will figure out the best strategies to put in place and help the leadership team adopt Agile at individual level and at business unit, country, regional or global level.

Establish an Agile Center of Excellence (ACoE/ACE)

When you plan enterprise agility across the organization, you need the Agile experts/ practitioners who know the subject in detail to do this job. If we talk about a small Agile team, it has a scrum master and product owner as the minimum resources who are specialized in Agile. Now multiply this with the number of teams you have across the entire organization. That means if your organization has 1,000 employees and all of them are running in small Agile teams, we are talking about approximately 100 scrum masters and 100 product owners. However, at the very beginning, all the organization may not be transformed into Agile, hence it is possible that the number can be fewer than that. Also, depending on the maturity, internal employees will also be able to be scrum masters and product owners and that should be the goal.

That means during this transformation process, your organization will develop 'Agile capital'. That will consist of your organization's 'Agile body of knowledge', Agile experts like scrum masters, Agile coaches, teams, trainers, etc., and processes and tools. They will need to create a community to discuss the subject area and develop themselves in Agile. That can be done by establishing an Agile Center of Excellence (ACE).

The ACE owns the success of the Agile transformation in the organization. It will be sponsored by the chief executive officer (CEO) and will be led by the chief agile officer (CAO). All Agile professionals like Agile consultants, trainers, scrum masters, product owners, DevOps consultants and trainers will belong to the ACE. And they must be accessible to anyone in the organization at any time because they are the change agents and counselors of Agile practice.

Hack the Culture

As we discussed in the previous sections, 'being Agile' requires changing the culture of the organization and the way people work. One of the reasons Agile fails is when this behavioral and cultural aspect of the change is forgotten or deprioritized. You cannot hire Agile practitioners like Agile coaches, scrum masters, and product owners and get the teams to follow Agile practices, only to ask them to follow the old processes you have been using.

In the ServiceNow ITSM implementation, which I referred to earlier, once the Agile way of working was established, the PMO and the COO who ran the steering committee expected me to produce PowerPoint presentations every week to report the progress of the committee. When I provided a lightweight presentation with just the essential details, the very first comment I got was that the PowerPoint presentation did not follow their branding guidelines and the color combinations were wrong. That almost made me crazy as, by that time, more than 1.6 Million AUD had been spent, there were only two more months before the go-live, the teams were putting in an enormous amount of effort to recover the program, and we were making progress thanks to the Agile way of working, yet the CIO wanted the presentations to be in the perfect color coding!

At that moment, I walked straight to the CIO's office and gave him two options. I showed him the backlog of the work that had to be finished by the team and me and then the efforts required to get the perfect PowerPoint he needed. If my team or I had to get the PowerPoint branding right, we would have to deprioritize something else from the product backlog and I asked him to do that prioritization for us. He then got the idea. We agreed to scrap the entire steering committee and he and his steering committee attended the product showcase to see the progress instead of the team spending time on producing status update reports at the cost of team burnout. With these changes, we could get the project back on track and deliver it on time.

Another example is a start-up I was coaching. The team was constantly bombarded with ideas coming from the CEO. The CEO, inspired by light bulb moments, kept on feeding his ideas to the team and expected those ideas to be implemented literally by the next day or week. When it was not done, he pulled his team into impromptu meetings and explained the ideas so that they could implement them quickly. The team, who joined the company with high enthusiasm, lost motivation very soon as they did not even get a chance to finish the work they started because the CEO kept on pushing new ideas to be implemented, which he then abandoned when he had another idea. Finally, they started leaving the company one by one until it was half its previous size. And the funny thing was that this CEO promoted Agile at team level and expected the team could do magic just because they were following Agile.

These are anti-Agile patterns originating from the leadership level. Changing these anti-Agile patterns is not an overnight job. Transforming unproductive organizational behavior requires effort, but it can be done one step at a time.

Jeff Bezos is famous for the many culture hacks he introduced at Amazon, revolving around the 12 leadership principles they developed. Let's take, as an example, Amazon's first leadership principle, 'Customer obsession'. Now how does Jeff Bezos showcase that across the organization? If you read books or articles about Amazon or ask a leader working there, they will give you the answer. According to these sources, when hosting leadership meetings, Bezos often left an empty chair to represent the 'customer' and remind everyone that the purpose of the company is to deliver value to the customer and the customer's opinion and ideas should be considered.

These small changes are like vitamins. Even a small dose takes the organization a long way. When you are the leader, people tend to follow you and you can influence these small culture hacks that make a huge impact in the long run. At one of the organizations I coached, the CEO introduced the 'no more than three slides in a presentation' policy. Prior to that, everyone, including the CEO, used to create PowerPoint presentations with twenty to thirty slides. Sometimes they even hired PowerPoint developers. Just before the monthly executive meeting, all the C-level leaders and their team members would go into panic mode trying to create PowerPoint presentations for a 40-minute meeting. But not all the slides they created were used in the meetings. After adopting Agile, the CEO decided that PowerPoint presentations were not only a waste of time, but they also did not improve people's face-to-face communication and articulation skills. Hence, he introduced the 'less PowerPoint more collaboration' policy and walked the talk.

In almost all the companies I've been involved with, I introduced the 'out by five' policy when I had the authority to do so. I've noticed in many Asian countries, people stay until the boss leaves, taking on loads of work and working well into the night. As a result, they leave the office late. When they return to work the next day, they are drowsy, often agitated, and lack energy. That negatively impacts the work.

There needs to be quality over quantity. Hence, I started making everyone leave the office by 5 pm, maximum by 5:30, and when someone did not leave, I went to their desks and pulled the plug. That gave them a big hint that we were not measuring the number of hours. Instead, their wellbeing, spending time with family and their social network outside the office was important to be productive within the short period of seven to eight hours in the office. That also helped them to focus and time box the work because they knew they were not going to stay long hours in the office. This simple culture hack changed the employees' productivity and happiness drastically.

So, as a leader, how can you bring these small changes to the organization? How can you implement culture hacks that will help your organization become Agile? The surprising thing is that hacking culture is simple and easy. But it needs to be a gradual process and it needs to start from the leadership level, that is, you.

7

AGILE CENTER OF EXCELLENCE (ACE)

W hen an organization is thinking about developing and operating using Agile as a way of doing things horizontally and vertically across the organization, it comes with the necessity of developing Agile capabilities, knowledge capital and practitioners in the form of subject matter experts in the organization. Thus, it is logical and essential to establish an Agile Center of Excellence (which can be named any other way the organization wishes to brand it).

Imagine an organization with 20,000 or more employees in one or multiple geographical locations. One reason they may think of implementing or operating using Agile across the organization is to plan and be ready for future growth. And when the company achieves the targeted growth, then other requirements will arise, requiring new approaches. Agile is never a destination; instead, it's a journey.

An Agile Center of Excellence takes the ownership to lead the organization through this journey from infancy to maturity. It may not be necessary for all organizations to have their own Agile Center of Excellence. For example, a small organization with 10,000 or fewer employees may not need one. But when the number of employees and stakeholders increases, an ACE becomes a necessity.

ACE Stakeholders

When Agile is implemented across an organization, the implementation involves multiple stakeholders directly and sometimes indirectly. Some stakeholders are beneficiaries while others are drivers, or as I call them, Agile transformation agents.

The beneficiaries, like customers, are those who will receive the benefits of the Agile implementation. Generally, it's recommended that customers collaborate in the Agile process, hence it may not be 100% accurate to say customers are outside the process and at the receiving end as beneficiaries. However, in most cases, customers are at the receiving end. Imagine a COVID-tracing mobile application developed by the Department of Health, which is operating using Agile. The public may not be directly involved in the process, although they contribute by providing feedback on the app and probably doing testing, hence they are at the receiving end.

Indirect contributors are the people who will not be directly involved in the Agile work but involved when required. In the above Department of Health example, the CIO or the digital officer may not be directly involved but they may be indirectly contributing by providing the necessary sponsorship and leadership commitment.

Agile drivers or active contributors are the people who drive the Agile transformation across the organization. I name them Agile transformation agents.

Agile Transformation Agents (ATAs)

ATAs are the drivers of Agile in the organization. They possess a theoretical and practical body of knowledge relating to Agile values, principles, practices, tools, processes, and frameworks and are thought leaders with practical experience. Their representation is at different levels of the organization at team, business unit and enterprise level.

Scrum masters, team-level Agile coaches, enterprise-level Agile coaches, Agile consultants, and Agile trainers are all ATAs. Some of them may have vertical specializations, such as Scrum framework or Kanban. However, enterprise-level ATAs have horizontal specializations with knowledge of many frameworks, programs, projects, and experience in different sectors.

While in-depth Agile knowledge is required, other cross-functional knowledge and skills such as change management, human behaviour, leadership, communication, and strategic leadership are also required to lead organizational-level Agile transformations.

ATA representation at different levels

Depending on where Agile is applied, such as enterprise, business unit or team level, Agile transformation agents may be required. When implementing Agile at business unit or enterprise level, the leaders at the strategic level should adopt Agile ways of working, culture, values, and mindset. The ATAs at leadership level help the rest of the leaders with the necessary coaching and mentoring.

However, most organizations have not paid enough attention to the importance of ATAs at the strategic leadership level. What we have seen is that ATAs are available at every level except strategic leadership level. This may lead to hindrances if leaders continue to plan and operate in an anti-Agile manner, as in the ServiceNow implementation example above. In the 15th annual State of Agile report, lack of leadership participation in Agile processes was identified as one of the top five challenges organizations face when implementing Agile. (Digital.ai Software, 2021) Forty-one percent of the participants in this research mentioned this and it is aligned with other empirical research conducted.

It is necessary to have Agile experts at the leadership level who can speak the same language as executive leaders to get them to transition to Agile. Sometimes very experienced Agile coaches can do that, but the majority only help at the team, program, or business unit levels. They may be lacking executive leadership level knowledge, which can be an issue. Recently I had a conversation with a chief digital officer at a global sports shoe manufacturer that has adopted Agile across all the business units, such as supply chain, finance, etc. All the business units are Agile, moving fast, but at the strategic leadership level everything is slow. They want to do the budgeting, strategic planning, and portfolio planning in the Agile way, but the existing Agile coaches have not managed to help them. As the chief digital officer said, "They don't get the language, and sometimes they don't understand the concepts like portfolio planning." So, although the leadership team badly wants to move to the Agile way of working, they are not able to do that.

Hence, it is necessary to have someone at the top with enough leadership experience who can motivate, influence, and challenge the executive leadership to move to the Agile way of working and that person is the chief agile officer.

Chief Agile Officer (CAO)

The chief agile officer is a strategic leadership member whose main responsibility is to drive enterprise agility operations across the entire organization. The CAO owns the Agile practice and is accountable for Agile's implementation in all the divisions of an organization. Working with the strategic leaders, the CAO proposes how, when and what Agile frameworks and practices need to be deployed for each division or unit of an organization.

The CAO owns the Agile strategy and implementation roadmap, which explains how and when Agile will be implemented gradually through the entire organization. The CAO reports to the CEO like any other C-level leader. Without that level of authority and accountability, enterprise level change is impractical due to the high level of resistance.

Figure 33: The Chief Agile Officer is the center point
of an organization's Agile transformation journey

The CAO's skill set

The job of chief agile officer requires a combination of various skills, capabilities, and cross-functional knowledge. They need to be capable of driving behavioral and cultural changes and implementing change management strategies, as well as have skills relating to human psychology, negotiation, and communication. They need the ability to influence others with different mindsets, including those who have authority in the organization. Such skills and capabilities are essential as at enterprise level, multiple challenges arise, and each business unit may have different cultures and operational styles. For example, a finance department may be risk-averse, while sales and marketing may be very open to changes if they bring about a reduced cycle time. Different strategies may need to be applied to risk-averse business units. Imagine a supply chain director who owns the supply chain strategy and has been in the company for 25 years. She may not be ready or convinced by the Agile way of working and will not move a pin in the department to go in that direction. The CAO should have very good leadership skills to figure out ways to convince the resistant leader to come on board.

Vast knowledge of Agile frameworks, practices, theories, tools, and techniques is essential for a CAO. An organization with hundreds or thousands of employees and multiple business divisions spanning across countries and regions may require different Agile frameworks and processes. Scrum may work on one occasion, but it may require extreme programming in another situation. Nexus framework may be required in one country, while Spotify may be needed for another department or enterprise level. Extensive Agile framework knowledge will help the CAO to select the best frameworks to suit different business unit requirements.

Also, it may even be necessary to develop a unique Agile framework, set of values, practices, and metrics suitable for the organization rather than trying to implement other frameworks. But to do that requires a huge amount of in-depth knowledge about everything described in the previous paragraph.

Strong business acumen and broad knowledge of the different business functions or units will be a must for the CAOs as they are required to have conversations with these business leaders and units and support them in the transition. Having a decent knowledge of how supply chains and financial models work or the legal system will help to have meaningful discussions with the relevant leaders. Someone with a visionary and strategic leadership style who can see how the organization will look after the Agile transformation is essential so that other leaders will buy into the Agile way of working and support it.

Clear communication, coaching and mentoring abilities are other must-have skills for a CAO. With appropriate coaching and mentoring, the CAO will be able to convince the other leaders to consider the net benefits the company stands to gain through Agile. In addition, this skill set is important because Agile implementation means that some of the executive leaders will need to be coached and mentored on leadership styles applicable under Agile.

The CAO must have the above skills, knowledge, and leadership as they take the lead in strategizing, planning, and executing the responsibilities outlined below.

Developing a vision and strategy for Agile Implementation

Agile is a culture, a mindset, and a new way of doing things. It will change the way things are done when it is applied at the level of teams, business units, and the enterprise. It may even significantly change how the organization is structured. The CAO should be able to develop a vision, then articulate and create a strategy to materialize that vision. As we've seen, in many cases, organizations want to achieve agility and nimbleness at enterprise level. That means the organization needs to focus on value delivery and respond to changes swiftly. This vision for enterprise agility needs to be developed with the collaboration of other C-level leaders. A vision that is futuristic but achievable will be motivating enough so that others will jump on board to execute it.

Setting Up an Agile Center of Excellence

Depending on the level of investment and size of the organization, the ACE can be a standalone unit or the subdivision of another unit. For example, if the organization has a separate department or unit such as a 'transformation office,' which adopts practices like Six Sigma, ISO etc., then the ACE can also be part of this unit as a separate function. However, if the organization is large, say 100,000 employees scattered across many countries, then making the ACE a separate function, office or division in each country makes more sense.

Once established, the ACE can take the following approaches to accelerate the Agile journey in the organization:

- Create a roadmap and strategy to expand Agile in the organization
- Develop Agile governance
- Enable the ACE by training and coaching to develop the capabilities
- Identify, initiate, execute, and support pilot projects
- Utilize lessons learnt to accelerate Agile maturity
- Develop metrics and measure the success against the roadmap metrics

- Continue Agile expansion throughout the organization horizontally and vertically.

Developing an Agile roadmap

Most enterprise-level business leaders are convinced that they need to move to the Agile way of working. But almost all of them become stuck in the dilemma of how to scale it up, how to measure the success, and where to begin. They question if the investments will yield any benefits or work in their context. These dilemmas can be addressed by developing an Agile roadmap for the enterprise. This will include the steps below, although many other sub-tasks may exist:

- Assessing the Agile status and maturity
- Creating new Agile business use cases
- Proposing a cost-benefit analysis
- Creating a capability plan.

Organizations are complex, complicated and have different operating models. Hence, one Agile framework does not suit all. The Agile way of working needs to start from somewhere, and it may be small and incremental or a large, big bang approach. Whichever Agile path is chosen, a planned and data-driven approach is needed. This encompasses an assessment of the current state of Agile (if it is applied in the organization at all), the plan for the transition state, and the future state. When deciding the transition and future states of Agile, tools like the Stacey Matrix can be utilized, although different ATOs may use other tools (the tool used is not as important as the outcome).

Tools such as the Stacey Matrix can help to understand factors contributing to the complexity of the organization and choose the best management actions to address different degrees of complexity. As an example, there are certain business use cases where stakeholders agree about the expected outcome. Such business use cases can be treated as simple or less complicated. They are low hanging fruits and can be started quickly using proven simple Agile frameworks like Kanban or Scrum. My example of the recruitment of engineering resources falls into this category as we knew what we wanted to achieve in terms of outcomes, and the stakeholders from HR and customers were aligned.

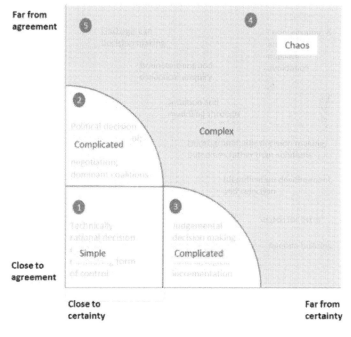

Figure 34: Stacey matrix

However, some business use cases are complicated due to uncertainty about the outcomes or because the stakeholders are misaligned. Such use cases fall into the category of complicated areas which need to be structured using exploratory approaches such as Scrum or Large-scale scrum frameworks. The example of M-Company (implementing Service Now ITSM) falls into this category as the outcomes required were certain, but the multiple stakeholders were not in alignment.

Complex or chaotic business use cases require more leadership engagement, drive, support, and multiphase approaches, which usually combine different tools like design thinking, business modelling, Scrum, SAFe, Nexus, Spotify and other applicable disciplines. Large enterprise-level programs, new product introductions, and business-unit-level Agile implementations may fall into this category depending on the size of the enterprise, industry and the organization's culture.

Developing an internal Agile framework

Some Agile frameworks may suit the company and the operational structure better than others. It may also depend on the type of business. As an example, Kanban or Scrum can be applied in all situations, but when it comes to scaling up, it's necessary to decide which framework suits the organization or the unit best. SAFe may work for enterprise solutions or capability development, while Nexus may be suitable for new product introductions, and Spotify may be how the organization wants to operate. Or the organization may need to develop its own framework as a long-term, strategic solution because each organization is unique with different operational challenges. Hence, the ACoE/ACE should ideate, research, prototype, and design the best framework for the organization. That does not mean it is necessary to scrap the other frameworks completely. It simply means combining and integrating best practices and models to develop customized and suitable frameworks.

One of the biggest mistakes most organizations make is copy pasting frameworks like SAFe or Spotify. One organization that tried implementing SAFe as the framework for their strategic program developed the program increment (PI) planning as instructed by the SAFe handbook; they did two days of PI planning with the entire organization. Their planning started at 8:30 am and ran until 5 pm, exactly as instructed by the SAFe PI planning calendar. However, this company operates in two countries: USA and Australia. The leadership team was in the USA, while the operational and development teams were in Australia. When it came to operationalizing the PI plan, it was not possible to get results because the leadership team could not be available to do the business review in Australian time when the teams finished their day. As a result, the entire planning had to be scrapped.

It is, therefore, important for an Agile Center of Excellence to research or find out what framework, existing or custom-made, works best for their organization.

Developing Agile product/service portfolios

One of the functions of the ACoE/ACE is to develop product and service portfolios that other business divisions can utilize.

For example, it should have a defined Agile blueprint for program and project management, product development, etc., including training materials, the training agenda, a handbook for managers and Agile leadership principles. These Agile portfolios should be useable as blueprints by other divisions. For example, Agile marketing can be used by the marketing division.

Collaboration with other units and leaders is essential as input and insights must come from them. The solution needs to work for them so that they are keen to give it a try. But it is also important that constant support is provided as part of these offerings. As Agile is new for them, just providing a set of artifacts and leaving them alone will not work out.

Developing an Agile workforce

Behind every successful Agile transformation, there are incredible scrum masters, Agile coaches, or consultants. And any enterprise Agile transformation needs plenty of them. The ACoE/ACE leads the initiative to develop this human and knowledge capital required to lead the Agile transformation of the organization.

The CAO's strategy should include how this human capital is built, and then gradually make every individual in the organization a scrum master, product owner, and an Agile leader who lives and breathes the Agile values, mindset, and principles. At the beginning stage, when the organization is completely new and starting the Agile Center of Excellence from ground zero, the CAO may decide to hire this human capital from the external world.

If the CAO decides to do that, a partnership should be built with this external company or consultants and within an agreed period of time, the internal employees should be trained and coached in such a way that gradually capabilities are built internally and people within the organization share the same knowledge and experience as external consultants. When hiring people from the external world, their cultural fit with the organization and leadership skills needs to be considered. As explained previously, transformation work like Agile needs more leadership skills than anything else.

One of the organizations I worked with appointed a selected candidate from each department (human resources, finance, logistics, etc.) for an apprenticeship for two years where they got coaching, mentoring, and training with the CAO and other staff in the ACoE/ACE. That helped to get the functional knowledge of the business units into the ACoE/ACE to develop better Agile methods. And once the apprenticeship finished, they went back to their respective units, where their job was to start transforming the business unit. It was successful as the others in the business unit listened to this person as it was someone with functional knowledge of their unit.

The Agile practitioners in the ACoE/ACE can be fully deployed to other units, projects, or programs to help them. For example, when the operations department tries to implement Agile, an Agile coach, scrum master, or a product owner can be deployed to the operations department full time so that the department has their involvement from the very beginning.

Developing Agile metrics

How do we measure the agility of the organization? Is the organization on the right track on the Agile journey? How do we know if it is on the right track or not?

One of the important jobs of the ACoE is developing a framework which consists of key performance indicators at the organizational, business unit, and other operational levels. These KPIs at different levels are required as each will be working toward different outcomes. At enterprise level these metrics may look like the number of units fully operating in Agile, the number of people trained in Agile, the number of projects done in Agile, the number of Agile release trains, and the number of Agile professionals trained in the organization (or in the ACoE). In the IT organization, it may be the number of IT product releases, the amount of time taken to release a product, the number of product defects, resolution time, the number of Agile projects, etc.

This needs to be measured against the organizational KPIs such as CAPEX and OPEX. In addition, at business unit level it needs to be measured against the business unit's strategic KPIs. As an example, the HR unit may have a strategic KPI like hiring new employees within two weeks instead of 12 weeks. The Agile way of working or the cross-functional collaboration or new Agile operating style may contribute to achieving these business unit KPIs. If the time to hire increases from 12 weeks to let's say 16 weeks after Agile implementation, then definitely something is wrong (although there may be other factors to consider, for example a niche skill set). So, the effectiveness of Agile needs to be measured by comparing the data prior to implementation and during the implementation.

Facilitating Agile tool selection

One of the very first questions I have always been asked in Agile consultation is "What tool should we use?" Undoubtedly, selecting the right Agile tools is important, but tools are not going to solve the problems. Tools need to be used as an aid and not as the main method of Agile implementation.

The companies or start-ups developing these tools are doing an amazing marketing job to the level that organizations and leaders feel that their projects or organizations are failing because they have not adopted these specific tools. To be clear, just adopting tools is not going to save your failing projects or programs. In fact, if not properly done, these tools will make things worse. No tool can solve the problem, but you can solve it with the right process, people, user experience and business processes, along with the tools.

In my Agile career, I have run more than seven different large programs with a value of more than two million USD each, without a single tool. No Jira. No Asana. No Monday. com. Just physical Kanban walls at different levels and people and the right processes were enough to deliver those programs on time, on budget with value to the customer.

One of the Australian banks I worked few years ago operated a Project Management Office (PMO) without a single technology-based tool. The PMO ensures all the programs were delivering their agreed outcomes on time and within budget. Some programs were regulatory programs where the reporting lines linked to the commonwealth government. The PMO managed 15 different programs worth more than 75 million AUD. Operated using fully Agile, the only tool they used was a visual program level Kanban board which was set up on one of the walls in the building, and Agile practices like quarterly program planning, standups, showcases and retrospectives. None of the programs used any IT tools which are in the market, and it was not simply required as all the leaders, program managers, project managers, and program teams, including the business were operating using those Agile practices.

However, when the programs are large and involve multiple regions, then the right tools and technologies (for example, video conferencing) are required to mitigate the hindrances caused by geographical barriers.

Once the tools are selected, the ACoE/ACE should take the lead by owning the tools and developing the capabilities to use the tools according to the ACoE/ACE process planning across the enterprise. The ACoE should develop training materials and training to use the tool in the right way to get the expected outcomes.

Influencing and Helping Other Business Units to Adopt Agile

Agile transformations across enterprises are hard, especially in large organizations. Often pushbacks will be stronger than support and enthusiasm, particularly from the leaders. These pushbacks can be explained by the 'diffusion of innovation theory' (Rogers, 2003). According to this theory, the adoption of any new process, technology, or innovation varies over a period of time. Some people will be quick to adopt the innovation or technologies and others will take some time to jump on board. And there is another portion of late adopters who take a long time to get convinced and a portion who will never adopt these new ways.

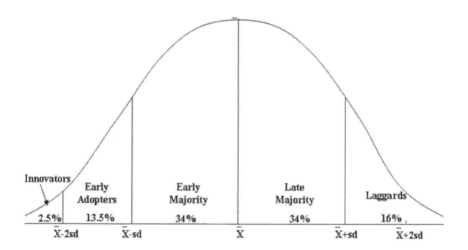

Figure 35: The diffusion of innovation (Rogers, 2003)

Different strategies are required to get people on board with the change based on where they are in the spectrum. For example, those who are very late may wait to see how others' journeys have been and may need influence from others through success stories to be convinced. Those in the innovators and early adopters' portion can be used to influence others as they may have good lessons to share, which others can benefit from.

The practitioners of the ACoE/ACE and the CAO should figure out the best strategies to get others to join the Agile transformation journey.

Developing an Agile Community of Practice

When an organization starts practicing Agile, Agile knowledge will start to proliferate. As each business unit and the leadership teams operate using Agile, many lessons will be learned. However, for example, the firm's IT department might be using Agile practices and frameworks such as Scrum and DevOps and the human resource or operations departments may use Kanban, so their lessons and challenges may be very different. Their knowledge will be isolated unless the CAO finds a way to collect it, develop it and use it to help others.

This is where Agile communities of practice (ACoP) come into the picture. ACoP are social events organized by Agile professionals. Anyone can take the lead in organizing one. It may be a knowledge-sharing session, a demonstration, or a problem-solving event. As an example, let's say the HR department wants to find out how they can reduce end-to-end time to hire. They can bring this problem to the ACoP and someone with good facilitation skills can do an ideation session or value stream mapping session with the very diverse group of people who attend the session. Or maybe sales and marketing have tried out Scrum and they want to share the lessons learned.

These events do not necessarily need to be internal. External contributors or practitioners can be invited, and in that way, knowledge from the external world will flow into the enterprise. For example, a CEO of a start-up could come and share their experience of how Agile helped their company to become a thriving business. Because of their desire to learn, the employees and business leaders will listen with enthusiasm. The ACoE/ACE should, therefore, focus on increasing these external collaborations and redirecting a flow of knowledge into the organization.

Operate using Agile

In one of the companies where I worked previously, entering the ACoE/ACE office was like visiting a start-up in Silicon Valley. The center's physical appearance was in stark contrast to the other units of the organization. For example, the center had an open space with no partitions between the employees' desks. The desks were surrounded by physical Kanban boards, sticky notes with flashy colors, and posters with hand-drawn artworks describing Agile concepts. The space was decorated with live plants, and people sat on beanbags. At any given time, it was difficult to find anyone sitting alone. Instead, there were always at least two or three people chatting together at the whiteboard or Kanban wall. They wore T-shirts printed with their Agile branding, unlike employees in other divisions who wore corporate attire.

The other thing that was very noticeable was that those who worked in that department were a happy bunch of people. When someone new entered the center, they were always inquisitive about the difference in the center's environment. This, on its own, was a form of influence and an opportunity to show to others that there is a new and better way to work and make money: the Agile way. So, an ideal ACoE/ACE must live and breathe Agile, especially in its operations, so that others can be convinced it is a practice worth giving a trial. The ACoE/ACE unit should be a role model for true agility in the organization, operating and living by the Agile values, manifesto, principles, and practices.

8

FOOD FOR THOUGHT

AGILE is not a Ferrari

As part of the research for this book, I surveyed 33 executive leaders in global professional services, IT companies, oil & gas companies and asked why they wanted to adopt Agile across their organizations. Ninety-five percent of them wanted Agile to help with the acceleration of outcome deliveries of projects, programs, or other initiatives. Many other executive leaders expect similar results.

Agile is associated with speed, and the general perception is that it will expedite the outcome deliveries. This image may be shattered, resulting in disappointment when Agile fails to deliver in this respect. Generally, this is a case of misguided expectations.

Agile has not been designed and developed to make things faster. The whole purpose of Agile is to increase 'value delivery to the customer'. In the process of delivering value to the customer, Agile focuses on reducing waste by minimizing the activities that produce waste and focusing on activities that yield value.

As an example, in the ServiceNow project for M-Company, discussed earlier in the book, activities like presentation-driven steering committee status updates or project team members working on parallel projects, etc. were non-value delivering activities. As a result, the team could not deliver anything tangible within the agreed time even though they were overworked. Replacing those non-value-added activities with value-driven activities (such as leaders attending the sprint showcases to get updates and making the team members dedicated to just one project) accelerated the value delivery, which can be interpreted as faster delivery. Speed was a by-product instead of the main goal of the Agile process in that situation. If there is not the right amount of focus on identifying waste and adding value-delivering activities, Agile will not be able to make things faster miraculously.

What needs to be understood, especially at the leadership level, is that enterprises may have many processes, practices, and structures which hinder value delivery. Unless leaders are open-minded about identifying these and replacing them with value-delivering processes, practices, and structures, Agile will not deliver leaders' expected outcomes.

Agile cannot fix all your problems

You cannot take a tomato seed, drop it in the middle of a desert and visit with a basket one year later, expecting a harvest. The tomato seed is Agile in this context, and the desert is the enterprise environment. To proliferate and reap the benefits, Agile needs to be planted in the right environment, nurtured, and cared for. This includes weeding out unhealthy habits, practices, structures, and cultivating healthy ones. This is the way to achieve long-lasting results.

Most leaders expect Agile to do miracles even in the wrong environment, project, or industry. For example, it would be naïve to say that Agile can be used in a construction project to build a sky rise building like Burj Khalifa in Dubai. It may be possible. But no one has done it yet, hence we don't know. However, there may be some aspects, phases, or areas where Agile can be used in similar setups. Perhaps some Agile concepts or practices could be applied in the planning or designing phases of similar construction projects.

There are areas and industries where Agile has showcased clear and concise better results. However, the areas where it has not been widely applied and for which there are no academic references need experimentation. Take the case of Energy3000, which was a completely new area. Thinking about the Agile way of working in that context was perhaps somewhat insane, but the experimentation produced an outstanding result. There are many such examples with empirical evidence where Agile has been experimented with in unconventional areas or industries, yielding promising results. But rather than blindly applying Agile everywhere, an entrepreneurial mindset is required to apply Agile in other sectors or areas. That is where the Agile Center of Excellence can help by designing those experiments or pilots and evaluating the results *before* more investment is poured in.

Replacing old names with Agile terminologies is NOT Agile

Before you continue reading further, do a YouTube video search for 'The Backwards Brain Bicycle' and watch until the end. As it explains, learning one of the most fundamental things like riding a bicycle can be really complicated when we have learned it in a completely different way. Learning to 'be agile' is something similar. Overriding old habits with new habits is extremely challenging and that is what we have seen with many Agile implementation programs.

In one of the enterprise Agile transformations programs I worked on, I had a product owner, Janice, who was a product manager prior to starting Agile implementation. Janice was a high-profile manager ('Vice president – products'). She had 12 people reporting to her and was reporting to the general manager. Once Agile started, she was given a two-day training on Agile and the title 'Product owner'. During the Agile implementation, she had two jobs, the full-time product owner role and then the vice president job. Consequently, she had to attend other corporate meetings with other units.

She had a highly motivated Agile scrum team who were building a big digital banking product. The team worked using Scrum and were motivated and collaborated with each other. Since the team was moving fast, there were product increments or features which needed Janice's review or her approval to move to production. But Janice was not available when required because of her other engagements.

The team came to the office by 9 am and worked until around 5:30 pm. But they had to get the review feedback from the product owner, Janice, and she didn't come back to the team until around 6:30 pm after finishing all her other engagements. She sat with each team member and reviewed their work, giving any input required. After about three months, the team lost motivation completely. The reason? They were burnt out. They had been working from 9 in the morning until 5:30, and then they just waited and waited without going home. They went home around 8:30 or 9, and sometimes even later than that, once all the review work was done by Janice. Imagine that routine every day. And since Janice was their direct manager with a high rank and they were juniors in the organization, they were scared to talk about it. Clearly, they were thinking, "Why the hell can't she come and review the work before 5?" What Janice didn't apply in that case were the concepts of 'being a servant leader' and 'time boxing'.

We have seen in many Agile implementations that the project managers are renamed as scrum masters, the product manager is renamed as product owner, a program manager is renamed as release train engineer and so forth. In many of these cases, it is hard to see any progress being made even though huge investments are in place. One of the reasons is the reassignment of the same people into Agile roles without putting in place a proper assessment, coaching, and mentoring programs.

When Agile is implemented at scale, many of these roles change, and yes, some people who have been doing the old roles need to be moved into Agile roles. But it needs to be done with a lot of training, coaching, and mentoring. Just providing two days of training and expecting them to be servant leaders the next day isn't realistic. The Agile practices challenge the behaviors ingrained in us that we have been practicing for a long time. If you are a leader, try this in the next meeting you attend with your team. Just pay attention when you talk in the meeting. Are you the first one to talk, or are you the last one? What do you do when the other person says completely irrational things in the meeting? Do you feel like jumping in and correcting them?

Such behavior is difficult to break and needs very good coaching and leadership training and programs. In Janice's case, one-on-one coaching helped her understand how she was contributing to the team's demotivation. As she was coached, she was willing to accept it and change. However, there are some people who are just not ready to change. Ego, power plays and politics have a bigger stake sometimes. Hence, Agile role assignments need to be done carefully, based on behavioral assessments under the guidance of the Agile Center of Excellence.

Agile too can fail

According to the 2015 Chaos report published by the Standish group, even Agile projects have failed. However, the failure rates compared to the Waterfall methodology are low, as illustrated in the table 3. Their research sample is 10,000 customers, which can be considered quite a large data set to make conclusions based on empirical evidence.

SIZE	METHOD	SUCCESSFUL	CHALLENGED	FAILED
All Size Projects	Agile	39%	52%	9%
	Waterfall	11%	60%	29%
Large Size Projects	Agile	18%	59%	23%
	Waterfall	3%	55%	42%
Medium Size Projects	Agile	27%	62%	11%
	Waterfall	7%	68%	25%
Small Size Projects	Agile	58%	38%	4%
	Waterfall	44%	45%	11%

Table 3: Project success comparison

What is noticeable in this data is the correlation between project size and the failure rate. The bigger the project size, the bigger the chance of failure (though this remains low compared to the Waterfall method).

In our experience, this is due to the many reasons explained throughout the book. Large Agile programs and initiatives need many cross-functional integrations. For example, a big digital transformation in a retail company needs sales and marking, IT, finance teams, supply chain and human resource involvement in different proportions. While some departments like HR may have lower interaction, departments like supply chain or sales and marketing may have a high involvement along with IT. When a larger initiative across multiple units is required to adopt Agile, it throws up many challenges, so investment, commitment and leadership drive are a must. Without these elements, large Agile initiatives may not succeed.

Think before outsourcing

If you want a six pack, it is you who must do the work, not your personal trainer. The same applies to Agile.

Like many other initiatives, Agile outsourcing is quite popular. Many leaders and organizations depend on external service providers when doing Agile implementation across the organization. The reason for this is the lack of internal expertise and practitioners. Hence most management and IT consultancy companies get involved with such implementation initiatives.

However, Agile is an area where you need to be incredibly careful when outsourcing because with Agile what you are doing is changing the culture of the organization. External agencies cannot change the culture, although they can influence it, but they need the right capabilities and expertise to do that.

Working with and for consulting companies, I can say with confidence that only a few have the right level of expertise to help another company implement Agile. Some of these consulting companies have tried implementing the Agile way of working in their internal operations before advocating it to clients and other companies, so they do have the credibility to talk about what they promote. For example, if you've listened to some leaders from Pivotal Labs (acquired by VMware), you would have heard them talk about many things they practiced.

Pivotal Labs revolutionized software development, and they used Agile practices like pair programming, DevOps, and test-driven development. As a result, many companies got their expertise to revolutionize their IT development using advice from Pivotal Labs. I have met people who worked for Pivotal, and they proudly talked about how they used these modern practices internally. However, that is not the case for most of the professional services companies.

Most of these so-called Agile enterprise companies have not even implemented a single instance of Agile beyond their IT department. And even some of their IT departments are working in an incredibly old Waterfall way. They will be pushing you to transform your HR department using new methodologies and Agile, but their internal HR takes more than three months to hire one employee. Most of these professional services companies have only one thing in terms of Agile, that is, a bunch of people who have got various Agile certifications. They will boast about the number of certified scrum masters or SAFe-certified people they have. Yet, none of them have implemented any Agile programs or initiatives inside their own organizations. Certifications are nothing compared to practical experience.

The difference here is the cultural side of the transformation. If they have not thought about the cultural shift required for Agile transformation, they will not be able to manage when things get difficult. In one of the research projects I conducted, I engaged with a senior executive leader of SAP who explained to me why Agile implementations are difficult. According to her, "It is because of the change management aspects that we struggle to really move to Agile. We've already done lots of training, but our internal organization is too complex, and our clients are reluctant to change." Her clients in this case are the other internal departments. She was talking from her experience because she went through this change herself.

A bunch of gurus with a bunch of certifications will not be able to figure out how to tackle these situations if they have not implemented and gone through these cultural changes themselves. Hence, when hiring consulting companies, it's important to be extremely cautious. My suggestion is that you ask them to showcase how they have implemented Agile internally and the outcomes of that implementation. Their customers may be able to provide references, but it's even better if they can showcase, they have lived and breathed the Agile way of working in their own company. Instead of outsourcing the function, the best approach would be to create an ACoE/ACE, as I explained in the previous chapter. That would create the capabilities internally.

Role of Leaders in Agile

In many organizations, when working in the traditional, hierarchical manner, managers make decisions, and employees follow decisions. In other words, hierarchical organizations make more followers than leaders. And what is wrong with that? Well, it creates bottlenecks in the middle layer and the top layer of the organization, which limits swiftness and responsiveness. This could impact many enterprise-level metrics like customer experience, returning customers, customer loyalties, etc.

As an example, like millions of people, I gravitated to Amazon for online shopping, although hundreds of other online shopping providers serve in the region. And why is that? For me, it is because of the millions of products Amazon offers, the unbeatable delivery time (even during the COVID pandemic, it was the only company that managed to deliver the products the next day while many other companies made excuses for month-long delivery times), and their flexibility concerning returns (Amazon has refunded my money every time I made a complaint about a damaged product and the process is super easy). Purchasing on Amazon somehow contributes to making my life very easy. Amazon is achieving its target of 'delighting customers', at least in my case, and I know I'm not the only one who feels this way.

Providing such services to billions of people worldwide cannot be done by making followers. Customer care, delivery and warehouse people need to be able to make decisions on their own on a daily basis to create such scaled-up operations. The Agile way of working makes employees decision-makers, owners, and leaders rather than merely following their managers.

When the Agile way of working is implemented, previous managers and executives who used to have authoritative powers will now have a new role. They become servant leaders rather than authoritative leaders/managers. They are there to unblock employees' limitations. While the teams will take most of the responsibility to make things happen, the managers or leaders will see what is needed to support the teams. The insights will come from the team, project or program, business unit level retrospectives, stand-ups, scrum of scrums, product showcases, etc. Such events will give managers insights on hindrances the teams face, what is stopping them from delivering value or what obstructs their autonomy.

Managers/leaders need to find a way to get those insights without becoming a burden to the employees and then take ownership to find ways to remove blockers. For example, all the blockers identified at the stand-ups or scrum of scrums can be noted by the senior leaders and their job then becomes to resolve the blockers by the next day before the teams' stand-ups. When Agile is aggressively making progress, leaders/managers get to know their enterprise-level limitations, and this forces them to act swiftly to support the teams.

I propose the following approach for leaders, which allows leadership teams to be integrated into the Agile initiatives practiced by teams and at the same time, to practice Agile at leadership level.

How to help Agile teams?

Retrospectives give enough insights into what limitations teams face, and most are due to enterprise-level process hindrances. As an example, one team may say they cannot deliver on time because three people who resigned have not been replaced just yet and, as a result, their planned work cannot be completed. That indicates that there is an issue with the hiring process. Leaders/managers now can find a way to become aware of these blockers, make a backlog of them, prioritize as per the impact of not unblocking, and collaborate with the rest of the leadership teams in other functions to determine how to attack the problem. Specifically, they explore how to solve the problem so the same situation will not arise in the future. This process looks like the diagram below.

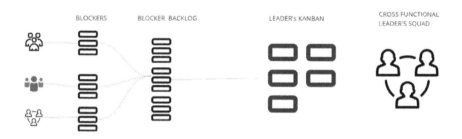

Figure 36 : Leadership squad and their backlog to find solutions

While some of these ideas can be implemented quickly by the leadership team, others may be strategic themes that need further ideation and strategic thinking. The items which need actions to stop teams from getting blocked need to be dealt with rapidly, but now they can also move forward quickly with other strategic themes as leaders have more time to work on them.

When solutions are not obvious, the leadership team can ideate with internal and external partners like recruitment agencies or explore other options they had never thought about, like hiring freelancers who are part of the gig economy. The results might be surprising and provide opportunities to be innovators in some areas.

Conclusion

Agile is many things. It is a way of working which maximizes value by reducing waste. It is a way to design an organizational structure, for example, using guilds, chapters, or Agile release trains. Agile is also a leadership development methodology, leveraging autonomy at individual and team levels. Hence, Agile at enterprise level can be applied and executed in many ways, depending on what the enterprise is trying to achieve. However, in order to reap the benefits at enterprise level, Agile needs to go beyond team level.

Implementing enterprise level Agile is a journey. Experimenting to find the optimal methodology requires patience and perseverance at every level of the organization. As the academic and empirical research studies suggest, achieving enterprise-level agility needs multiple frameworks, approaches, leadership commitment, and, most importantly, cultural changes. The need for leadership drive and to make Agile implementation a strategic initiative cannot be underestimated. The Agile way of working is the reason many organizations manage to thrive in an era where disruptions are unpredictable but constant.

REFERENCES

Alasad, H. (2020). The Impact of Agile Processes on Organisational Behaviour Within Current Banking Practice (Doctoral dissertation, Auckland University of Technology).

Bank, A. N. Z., Bank, P. P., & Panin, A. N. Z. (2013). Ownership Structure.

Binfield, H. J. I. (2018). Understanding Factors that Affect Design Knowledge Sharing Across Disciplinary Boundaries in Agile-Human-Centred Design Software Development Project Team Environments at ANZ (Doctoral dissertation, Swinburne University of Technology).

Bloomberg, J. (2016). How DBS Bank Became The Best Digital Bank In The World By Becoming Invisible. Forbes, pp. 1–5. Retrieved from https://www.forbes.com/sites/jasonbloomberg/2016/12/23/how-dbs-bank-became-the-best-digital-bank-in-the-world-by-becoming-invisible/?sh=4976d9b53061

Brosseau, D., Ebrahim, S., Handscomb, C., & Thaker, S. (2019). The journey to an agile organization. McKinsey & Company, May, 10.

Carlson, R., & Turner, R. (2013). Review of agile case studies for applicability to aircraft systems integration. *Procedia Computer Science, 16,* 469–474. https://doi.org/10.1016/j.procs.2013.01.049

Calnan, M., & Rozen, A. (2019). ING's Agile transformation— Teaching an elephant to race. Journal of Creating Value, 5(2), 190-209.

Digital.ai Software, I. (2021). 15th State of Agile Report. *Digital.Ai,* 1–23. https://stateofagile.com/#

Duran, Randall E., and Kevin Sproule. "DBS Bank: Championing change." (2012): 1-6.

Dennis, Pascal, and Laurent Simon. Harnessing Digital Disruption: How Companies Win with Design Thinking, Agile, and Lean Startup. Productivity Press, 2020.

Furuhjelm, J., Segertoft, J., Justice, J., & Sutherland, J. J. (2017). Owning the Sky with Agile. Building a Jet Fighter Faster, Cheaper, Better with Scrum.

Garton, E., & Noble, A. (2017). How to make agile work for the C-suite. Harvard Business Review, 19, 2017.

Jelassi, T., & Martínez-López, F. J. (2020). DBS Transformation (a): Becoming a World-Class Multinational Bank. In Strategies for e-Business (pp. 605-620). Springer, Cham.

Kien, S. S., Soh, C., Weill, P., & Chong, Y. (2015). Rewiring The Enterprise For Digital Innovation: the Case of DBS Bank.

Kerr, W. R., Gabrieli, F. E. D. E. R. I. C. A., & Moloney, E. M. E. R. (2018). Transformation at ING (A): Agile. Harvard Business Review, 1-19.

Lindlöf, L., & Furuhjelm, J. (2018). Agile beyond software-a study of a large scale agile initiative. In DS 92: Proceedings of the DESIGN 2018 15th International Design Conference (pp. 2055-2062).

Haworth, & Collectiv, W. (2017). *Raising the bar : Australian Millennials in the Workplace*. 1–19. https://media.haworth. com/asset/89200/Millennial Series: Raising the bar: Australian Millennials in the Workplace

Rigby, D. K., Sutherland, J., & Noble, A. (2018). Agile at scale. Harvard Business Review, 96(3), 88-96.

Rigby, D. K., Sutherland, J., & Noble, A. (2018). Agile at Scale: How to go from a few teams to hundreds. *Harvard Business Review, June*, 1–10.

Sia, Siew Kien, Christina Soh, and Peter Weill. "How DBS Bank Pursued a Digital Business Strategy." MIS Quarterly Executive 15.2 (2016).

Sergio da Cruz, P. (2000). *RESERVOIR MANAGEMENT DECISION-MAKING IN c Copyright 2000 by Paulo S ´ ergio da Cruz All Rights Reserved. March*. https://pangea.stanford.edu/ERE/ pdf/pereports/PhD/Cruz00.pdf

Xiuli Wang, Michael Economides, in Advanced Natural Gas Engineering, 2009

OTHER BOOKS
BY THE AUTHOR

Product Management in Agile Way

Agile Coaching

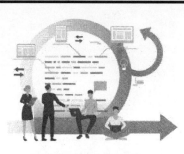

BECOMING A
SCRUM
MASTER

*Everything you should know to
be a GREAT Scrum Master*

ANUSHA HEWAGE

Agile Improvements

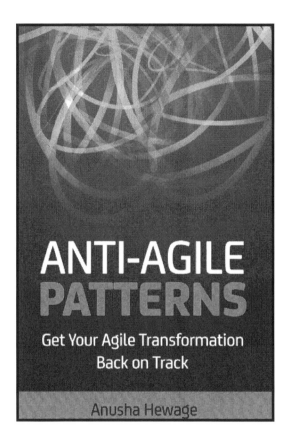

Made in the USA
Monee, IL
16 November 2022

17787345R00136